THE ART OF REAL ESTATE

Educate | Communicate | Inspire

THE INSIDER'S GUIDE TO BAY AREA

RESIDENTIAL REAL ESTATE

EAST BAY EDITION

BY

DEBBI DIMAGGIO & ADAM BETTA

The Art of Real Estate – Educate | Communicate | Inspire
The Insider's Guide to Bay Area Residential Real Estate – East Bay
Edition

Copyright © 2015

www.HalfFullPress.com
www.DiMaggioandBetta.com

Debbi DiMaggio – Author
Adam Betta – Author
Alison Mackey – Editor
Robert Bond – Publisher
Annie Barbarika – Graphic Designer

Kristen Malan – Book Cover
Quentin Bacon – Photography

Published in 2015 by:

Half Full Press
1814 Franklin Street, Suite 902
Oakland, CA 94612
(888) 612-9908

10 9 8 7 6 5 4 3 2 1

ISBN 978-0-9855036-6-6 | Printed and bound in South Korea.

To Our Amazing Children, Bianca and Chase,
May you both find a career that you are just as passionate about;
and excited to wake up to, each and every day.

With love,
Mom and Dad

Table of Contents

INTRODUCTION: ABOUT THIS BOOK

You hold in your hands the first installment of The Insider's Guide to Residential Real Estate series, an upcoming sequence of convenient and practical guides to area-specific real estate markets across the United States. In this San Francisco East Bay Area edition, interested local buyers and sellers will find area-specific advice from local real estate gurus Debbi DiMaggio and Adam Betta on navigating local market trends, choosing the ideal real estate partner, successfully marketing a home for sale, and managing financial concerns, among many other topics. The book also contains a myth-busting chapter that addresses common industry misconceptions from an agent's insider point of view, an exclusive interview with a local mortgage lender, a Glossary of relevant terms, and an extensive Appendix providing useful documents and relevant articles. This extremely localized guide, focusing on Debbi and Adam's major real estate markets in Piedmont, Berkeley and the Oakland Hills, is a must-have for any savvy buyer or seller looking to acquire or sell residential real estate in the area.

Perhaps you are already in the process of buying or selling in the San Francisco East Bay. Whether you are an East Bay homeowner who plans to sell one day, a first-time homebuyer looking to move into the area, or simply a curious consumer who wishes to learn more about the current climate of these local markets, you will find precise information, advice, and tips relevant to your situation within this Insider's Guide. While this book is generally geared toward individuals in the upper price points of their respective real estate markets, it is wholly accessible to any and all interested in educating themselves on "the art of real estate."

To get the most out of *The Art of Real Estate*, we earnestly recommend that you use it in conjunction with the professional services of a full-time, fully accredited, and thoroughly experienced real estate agent. No printed manual can hope to compete with the personal attentions and unparalleled services of living professionals like Debbi and Adam. While a terrific resource, this book cannot perform the services of an experienced Realtor®, and should rather be used to complement and reinforce the benefits you will receive from partnering with an agent.

Guide to Icons and Symbols

Spread throughout the book, you will find small graphic icons that indicate certain special features. These are: *"Technical Advice," "Research This!," "Rule of Thumb," "Local Insight," "Debbi Says...," "Don't Forget!," "Financial Pointer,"* and *"Warning."* The icons are found in the margins to the left of their corresponding text. In certain instances, a given icon may correspond to an entire chapter; in such cases, the icon is found in the upper left-hand corner of each page of that chapter. The diagram below illustrates the meaning of each icon. Pay special attention to these helpful visual symbols, and use them as markers to guide you on your journey through the text.

Technical Advice	Research This!	Rule of Thumb	Local Insight
Forms, details, documents, and more	*Something to check into in your spare time*	*Industry tips and tricks*	*Information specific to the East Bay*
Debbi Says...	**Don't Forget!**	**Financial Pointer**	**Warning**
Personal touches and suggestions from the author	*Important details that are often overlooked*	*Financial guidance and words to the wise*	*Common pitfalls or hazards to avoid*

Publisher's Note

Having just sold a home in a very hot seller's market, there are several key points that I feel are critical in buying or selling a home:

- All real estate is local and what might apply in one market most likely does not apply in other markets, even contiguous markets.
- Getting the most qualified and compatible agent (whether listing or buying agent) is essential in maximizing the value or minimizing the purchase price.
- Eliminating all the "unknowns" for a potential buyer greatly increases the purchase price. This means presenting the buyer with all the inspections and reports that a buyer would normally undertake on his or her own prior to closing. It also means that the house is ready to move into on Day 1, without the investment on the part of the buyer for painting, new carpets, new appliances, etc. In other words, leave nothing to chance.
- Staging, done properly and well thought-out, should generate well over the incremental cost of short-term storage and the stager's fees.
- Don't think you are smarter than the market, that you have all the answers and that you can successfully sell or buy a house without professional guidance. Trust your chosen agent to act in your best interests and, accordingly, follow his or her advice.

Let me note that I have been in and out of the real estate business for many years – two years doing limited partnership syndications, four years focusing on commercial property investments, and four years doing "spec" residential houses. Thirty-five years ago, we sold three homes that were meticulously updated and staged, without using a listing agent. Accordingly, I have a fairly good grasp of the underlying fundamentals of buying and selling properties. Unfortunately, times have changed in the intervening 35 years since I was involved with residential properties. The threat of litigation on the part of buyers has become a potential nightmare. Getting qualified contractors on your own in a seller's market is extremely difficult. Expertly marketing a property using social media, blogs, brochures, etc. is a field in itself.

My wife and I recently sold our home in Piedmont for a remarkable $850 per square foot. The 3-bedroom, 2-1/2 bath house had 2,500 square feet, a large yard by Piedmont standards, and a beautiful view of the San Francisco Bay and San Francisco. The listing agents were Debbi DiMaggio and Adam Betta. The listing price was $1,695,000. The home, which was staged, was on the market for only 10 days. (Our agents had set a pre-arranged offer date.) There were four offers over the asking price, the top offer being $2,110,000 – 24.5% over the asking price. Debbi unquestionably deserves the lion's share of the credit for the organizational and marketing skills she demonstrated in achieving the exceptional final results.

So how did we do this and, more importantly, how can you do this?

- We chose the hardest working, most marketing-oriented agents in the Piedmont Area. Although it was a difficult decision, we chose not to work with friends who were also real estate agents. We negotiated what we felt was a fair commission. We clearly stated what we expected from Debbi and Adam and agreed to follow their advice. I feel confident that they earned every bit of their commission through their focus and hard work.
- We followed their advice to the letter. This involved new carpets throughout the house, every surface freshly painted, wallpaper removed, a new furnace (the old one functioned, but was 35 years old), new appliances (some were over 30 years old), removing all wall hangings, etc. We also put in new sod in the front yard and black mulch in all flowerbeds.
- We had every inspection that a prospective buyer might want to see. This included a structural report, an electrical report, a chimney

inspection, a roof inspection, an HVAC inspection, water lines and pressure, sprinkler systems, landscaping, earthquake report, etc. We also had copies of all the building permits and city approvals for work properly completed. The buyer would not have to worry about improvements made without the necessary permits. We left nothing to chance that might cause a prospective buyer to worry about unforeseen and significant expenses after he or she moves in. Most buyers in a seller's market stretch to buy the "most" house they can and they certainly don't want to worry unnecessarily about putting in a new heater for $5,000 or a new roof for $20,000. Preliminary inspections on the part of the seller greatly reduce a buyer's level of anxiety and their need for time-consuming contingencies that delay closing at best and may preclude a sale at worst.

- After evaluating two bids from stagers, we staged the house – there was not a stick of our furniture left in the house. We learned from our agent just how important it is to neutralize the colors and furnishings in our home by staging, so as to appeal to a wide range of buyers. Buyers need to be able to visualize themselves living in the home, rather than seeing it as "our" home. My sense is that the $5,000 investment generated thousands more dollars in added value when it came time to sell.

My advice to a home seller is to always use a real estate agent with whom you feel comfortable and who has access to qualified contractors that are dependent upon future work with the agent. For the homebuyer, choosing the proper agent is equally critical, although more emphasis should be put on strong negotiating skills and the closing process and a thorough knowledge of the market in the area.

Rob Bond, Publisher
Half Full Press

ABOUT THE AUTHORS

Debbi DiMaggio is to real estate as Joe DiMaggio is to baseball: a charismatic winner with an exuberant style all her own. Debbi's reputation has spread from her native Piedmont throughout the Bay Area and the country, as a real estate professional in a class by herself. Her buyers love her tireless efforts to find them the right home and negotiate the best terms in any market, and her sellers can't imagine going through the process without her circumspect management of the entire experience. While Debbi makes her work appear effortless and even fun (a DiMaggio flair), this is by careful design, and is the result of years of experience and hard work. Passionate about what she does, Debbi partners with her clients to make the normally harrowing experience as seamless as possible. You will not only enjoy working with Debbi, but will benefit from her invaluable resources and connections in the real estate world.

For the past twenty plus years, Debbi has specialized in helping her clients relocate from across the globe, over the Bridge, and just around the corner. She focuses on a variety of East Bay neighborhoods, including, but not limited to: Piedmont, Oakland, Upper Rockridge, Rockridge, Crocker Highlands, Montclair, Redwood Heights, Oakmore, Berkeley, Albany, Alameda, El Cerrito and San Francisco, to name a few. With this depth of experience comes an intuition that enables her to usher her clients into environments and neighborhoods that seem almost designed for their specific needs and wishes. Debbi's reputation has resulted in a client list that reads like the credits of a Hollywood blockbuster, including such celebrities as Macaulay Culkin, Julianne Moore, Sally Field, Hugh Grant, Linda Fiorentino, Ted Danson, Tom Arnold and Jason Richardson. But whether you are a film star, professional athlete, philanthropist, entrepreneur, business owner, designer, CEO, teacher, firefighter or pastry chef, as Debbi's client, you are always the celebrity.

Like her famous relative (the world-renowned baseball player happens to be her third cousin), Debbi DiMaggio discovered early on what she does best. After graduating with a degree in Political Science from UC Berkeley, Debbi developed her natural talents to a high professional degree, making delighted clients the real winners. In addition to real estate, her life's passion, Debbi devotes her busy days to her many other interests: travel, family, charity work and design. Debbi is also the author of *contained beauty: photographs, reflections & swimming pools* (2012), a visual journey that captures her love of swimming pools, landscape, architecture, beautiful hotels and homes, writing, and people.

Adam Betta is perceptive, discerning and an excellent problem solver with over 21 years of experience. When Adam represents buyers and sellers—whether purchasing or selling a starter home or transacting their second or third high-end residential estate—Adam uses all personal and professional tools in his arsenal to ensure the best results for his clients. His close attention to detail coupled with his strong work ethic all enable him to continue a very successful career in real estate as well as to increase his pool of satisfied clients.

After receiving his real estate license in 1987, this fourth generation San Francisco native worked with buyers and sellers of residential properties in San Francisco. After meeting his wife and partner, Debbi, the two created and ran a leasing department prior to their move to the East Bay where Adam became a Broker Associate, once again selling real estate to satisfied buyers and sellers. Adam stepped over to the mortgage side of the business for a few years in order to sharpen his knowledge of the lending industry. In 2009 Adam returned to brokering with more to give to his clients as they are faced with today's rapid changes. Due to his training and immersion into the many facets of real estate, Adam is able to offer more knowledge and understanding to each of his clients.

Adam credits his degree in economics from The University of San Francisco for helping him find the right leverage in negotiations on behalf of his clients. His knowledge of rental property and leasing laws also make him well suited to advise clients in increasing the value of their income properties and homes. His experience in mortgage lending also helps his clients to understand more clearly the sometimes-complicated loan process and programs.

Relationships with his clients drive Adam the most. The experience of buying or selling real estate can be a very stressful and emotional process; therefore Adam takes particular care in walking clients through each step. Seeing an elated client signing their final papers is his favorite reward. In addition, Adam's meticulous work ethic, enthusiasm, patience and skillful negotiation have made him a favorite resource for current clients and new referrals.

Adam and Debbi have two children whom they absolutely treasure, a dog, named Biscuit, and parents who all live nearby. They both love family, community and serving others. Debbi spends quite a bit of time with her charity work and organizations, while Adam enjoys working with their children's coaches and sports teams. Although they both love to vacation, Debbi would rather be moving swiftly through the architecturally inspiring towns and villages of Italy and the South of France, while Adam treasures a vacation with no appointments. The two are very different, and yet, each complements the other; Debbi and Adam make a great team.

Together, Debbi and Adam have the skills, experience, and extensive knowledge—along with the magnificent team they have created and cultivated over the years—to help their clients enjoy maximum success whether as a buyer or a seller. Having had extensive training in the latest real estate marketing strategies and continually educating and training their agents, Debbi and Adam are confident that they can offer you knowledge and tools most other agents can't. Experience, integrity, and connections are key to making sure their clients succeed.

Contact this top producing team so they can keep you updated on the latest real estate activities in your community and answer any questions you may have. They look forward to assisting with all of your real estate needs for generations to come!

www.DiMaggioandBetta.com

Debbi's Unique Philosophy: the DiMaggio Difference

Educate | Communicate | Inspire

Most professional real estate agents view real estate as a career. For Debbi DiMaggio, real estate is a lifestyle and an integral part of who she is. As such, Debbi does not treat real estate as just any other job; instead, she brings a unique and personal philosophy to each of her transactions. Whether in her charity work or her real estate work, it is all the same: Debbi goes above and beyond the call of duty because she enjoys it, and not because it's her job. You will see for yourself: the DiMaggio Difference truly is an experience you won't find anywhere else.

Both Debbi and her business partner and husband Adam identify three critical factors that set them apart from their competition in the East Bay real estate world:

1. **Debbi and Adam both pride themselves on being extremely hands-on.** This means that they maintain an almost constant interaction with their clients, frequently checking in to address questions or concerns and holding their clients' hands throughout the entire buying or selling process. Every client has his or her own career to manage; for Debbi and Adam, this is their job – they will manage it smoothly for you as their client so that you can attend to other obligations. If Debbi is overseeing the renovation of a property, for instance, it is not uncommon to see her show up multiple times in a single day, managing over a dozen inspectors and/or contractors at a time. Both Debbi and Adam are committed to being thorough and promise to follow up frequently, providing data, second opinions, or whatever else will fulfill each client's individual needs. According to Debbi, real estate agents must also act as investigators and researchers – they are always out to protect their clients and are

constantly searching for the correct answers or a second opinion. If a question might be out of their area of expertise they will immediately look to the person who is the expert, whether this is a service provider, attorney, city official, or title officer. If you have questions, Debbi and Adam will obtain an answer.

2. **Debbi cultivates an extensive social media presence.** Debbi and Adam are fully aware that people spend their free time online – that's where clients are looking! To help keep her buyers and sellers connected, Debbi is especially active on Twitter, Facebook, Foursquare, Instagram, Pinterest, and several blogging platforms, where she skillfully executes all her clever—and highly successful—marketing ideas. Utilizing a variety of social media networks is an effective way of reaching all different age groups, since many different avenues connect you to many different people. Any seller wants to attract people to his or her open house, and Debbi knows that social media posts can be the invitation that draws buyers in. She therefore offers social media and marketing training to her fellow agents, so that it becomes second nature to them as well. You won't find this sort of media savvy anywhere else!

3. Lastly, unlike many other agents, when you hire **Debbi and Adam, you get *them***. Neither partner works with any assistants because they want to be present themselves, serving you the way they know best. Both agents bring something unique to the table that only they themselves can provide: while Debbi is the social media and marketing expert, Adam is the company's Broker, to whom many of the agents come for advice and, oftentimes, simple encouragement.

In addition to these three primary areas of focus which characterize the quality service both Debbi and Adam provide, the two pride themselves on many other industry insights and rare attributes.

- ❖ **Focus on Communication** – Attentiveness to her clients' needs is what sets Debbi apart. She considers communication the single most important and essential aspect of her line of work. She acknowledges that, in a real estate partnership, communication is all on the agent – all top agents must be facilitators, communicators, and educators by trade. In addition, communication in the modern era must happen speedily. Debbi and Adam never want their clients to have to wait around for answers, so both agents choose to be readily available at any hour of the day. While many older agents are unable to keep up with the fast pace of modern life and technology, Debbi feels that it is critical that she is on the same page as her clients in terms of communication. When you're buying or selling, you want your agent to be working at the same pace as you.

- ❖ **An International Presence** – Debbi and Adam are well respected and well connected across the state, the country, and the world. Debbi and Adam began their careers in San Francisco and maintain many contacts there, and they also network with a number of agents throughout the country and abroad through their affiliation with Who's Who in Luxury Real Estate, their international partner. They are happy to connect you with any one of the top Realtor® partners with whom they've collaborated over the years.

- ❖ **A Team Player** – Debbi is exceptional in viewing and treating her fellow agents as colleagues and collaborators, not as competitors. In her words, it's all about the clients, not about the agents. Debbi also understands the importance of forging lasting relationships with service professionals. She often calls on them for expert advice on various matters. Any agent is only as good as the cohort of service professionals she has working on her team, so Debbi maintains a stellar and devoted team of cohorts.

"

* ❖ **A Diverse Clientele** – Both Debbi and Adam are proud to deal in all price ranges. They treat all their clients with the same respect and commitment, no matter the price point; all clients are "luxury" clients and all are given equal amounts of their time and consideration. Debbi feels that price points don't matter because the money isn't of critical importance – for her, this work is a lifestyle and not a paycheck. Debbi's primary goal in working with her clients is the relationship, and not the monetary reward. (Don't get her wrong – like anyone else, Debbi works to make a living. But her clients do find it interesting to learn that she never calculates a commission or looks at her check at closing time. By then, she's already well on her way to helping her next client!)

* ❖ **A Strong Referral Network** – It is a testament to Debbi's integrity as an agent that, if she comes across a listing that falls outside her geographical area of expertise, she will always refer the client to a more knowledgeable local agent, rather than take on the job for herself. She prefers to make sure the client is provided for than to earn new business outside her own market; for this reason, Debbi maintains a very strong referral network both nationally and internationally. On the other side of the coin, it is a testament to Debbi's skill that she herself is frequently referred by other agents and companies who know that she and Adam together will get the job done successfully.

* ❖ **A Personal Touch** – Debbi takes all of her real estate transactions very personally. She empathizes with her clients in a way that virtually no other agent does. Debbi enjoys cultivating personal relationships. Every year, she invites all her clients and any new families in the neighborhood to enjoy the Piedmont 4th of July Parade from their Piedmont office. Bagels and coffee are provided! This is an example of Debbi's dedication to community, and her desire to bring

her clients into the close-knit fold of the community before they even move in.

In short, if you want a professional, communicative, connected, and shrewd real estate agent, you will find that and more in Debbi DiMaggio and her Partner, Adam Betta. Both Debbi and Adam hope that this real estate guidebook, unique in offering an insider's perspective on the specific East Bay micro-market, will help to prepare you for a successful home purchase or home sale. They look forward to assisting you personally.

CHAPTER 1: WELCOME TO THE SAN FRANCISCO BAY AREA

Alluring, magical, and indescribably beautiful, the San Francisco Bay Area draws millions of visitors each year. Those who know the area intimately might share their love and passion for the superb amenities, dynamic energy, breathtaking natural beauty, and unique cityscape as the area's major charms. When Fortune magazine ranked the San Francisco Bay region as number one for business nationally—and second worldwide behind Singapore—two of the primary factors cited were quality of lifestyle and the high concentration of intellectuals and entrepreneurs. Little wonder that Greater San Francisco invites comparison to other globally influential cities like Sydney, Rio de Janeiro, and Hong Kong.

In addition to the San Francisco and San Mateo counties, the San Francisco Bay Area consists of seven other counties: Alameda, Contra Costa, Marin, Napa, Solano, Sonoma, and Santa Clara. As you will discover, the entire region is a vibrant international community filled with the positive spirit of advancement, growth, and progress. Even though each community and neighborhood claims its own special character and charm, the Bay Area as a region offers an exciting and friendly, yet cosmopolitan, atmosphere. The greater San Francisco metropolitan region is also a magnet for new businesses seeking a location that combines economic vitality with an exceptional quality of life. The City of San Francisco joins San Jose and Oakland as the regional pulse points for business, commerce and distribution.

With more than seven million residents, the Bay Area ranks as one of the largest metropolitan regions in the country, claiming industries that range from high technology to high fashion. Stir in world-class universities, research laboratories, international markets, an exceptionally talented labor force and spectacular scenery. Add the high-tech leadership of the Silicon Valley, the prowess of San Francisco's banking and financial world, the innovation associated with Stanford University and UC Berkeley, and the industrial and distribution centers in Oakland. No other region in the nation brings together such superior ingredients in one relatively compact area.

With so many biotechnology research centers and eminent technological leaders—including such preeminent companies as Google, Facebook, Twitter, Pixar, Pandora, Square and Apple—the area is constantly forging new programs to support a highly educated workforce and a cultivated spirit of entrepreneurship. Top Bay Area companies now encourage a world-renowned state of health and wellness by offering bus and carpool services, gym and daycare facilities, and gourmet food to their hardworking employees. The "campuses" of these companies have become mini cities in their own right, where workers can feel comfortable working later and staying longer. In many sectors, though, telecommuting has become common practice, allowing Bay Area residents to live where they want to live rather than next door to their workplace. Thanks to the Bay Area's solid economy, many of its households boast high incomes. The region includes two of the top twenty-five wealthiest counties in the United States, and is one of the country's most expensive and desirable areas.

Services

Enhancing the industrial, commercial, and residential expansion of the area is an efficient transportation network of harbor facilities, international airports, rail services, highways and interstates, rapid transit, trans-Bay bridges and tunnels. For commuters who want to avoid highway and bridge traffic at peak hours, options for mass transit are abundant. Mobility is a top priority in San Francisco and throughout the Bay Area, constantly motivating planners and engineers to develop and maintain the finest of transportation amenities. San Mateo County, nestled at the very edge of San Francisco on the peninsula, is home to the San Francisco International Airport.

Newcomers to the Bay Area can look forward to a healthcare system that stands at the pinnacle of medical technology, staffed by some of the most brilliant, talented, and dedicated professionals in the nation. Quality diagnostics and treatment combine with cost-effective delivery of diverse services. Excellent healthcare systems ensure that a network of major hospitals, community clinics, advanced specialists and supportive services are available to meet every need.

World-renowned Stanford Hospital & Clinics assumes a leading role in healthcare advancements with highly acclaimed specializations that include the AIDS Research Center, Trauma Center, and internationally recognized cancer treatment programs. Nearby in Oakland, the UCSF Benioff Children's Hospital is distinguished as the largest, busiest and most comprehensive pediatric medical center between Los Angeles and Seattle. Throughout the regional and community facilities are proactive programs such as health screenings, fitness programs, and ongoing community education programs designed to safeguard and maintain good health.

Quality public and private schools serve the region, enhanced by a network of vocational and career institutions, community colleges, law schools and leading universities. The area boasts some of the West's most exceptional universities such as the University of California-San Francisco, Stanford University and the University of California-Berkeley. Community colleges combine with extensions for a number of California and national colleges and universities to bring higher education even closer to home. Most of these institutions provide flexible schedules that enable working adults to earn degrees while balancing a career and family responsibilities with the pursuit of a higher education or specialized skills.

Lifestyle

Imagine the quality of life available to newcomers to the San Francisco Bay Area, living each day in one of the world's most beloved tourist destinations. World-class museums, professional sports, spectacular gardens, lush parks and vast natural preserves ensure an unsurpassed quality of life. Around every corner, you'll discover a free music concert, an exciting attraction, or a chance to enjoy and appreciate nature. Attracting visitors from every continent, San Francisco places tourism at the top of its revenue-generating industries. The city creates a romantic, ever-changing and exciting atmosphere filled with memorable cultural, shopping, and entertainment opportunities.

Breathtaking vistas, stunning architecture, abundant parks, delicious restautants featuring almost any cuisine imaginable, impossible streets and quaint cable cars are all elements of San Francisco's enchanting ambiance. All four of the performing arts — symphony, theatre, opera, and dance — maintain celebrated permanent companies in San Francisco. Fine galleries mix with fascinating museums and science discovery centers, many that offer special programs and classes. The San Francisco War Memorial and Performing Arts Center covers a full seven acres in the heart of the city with dazzling venues like Davies Symphony Hall and the Opera House. Legendary museums such as the De Young, the San Francisco Museum of Modern Art, the Legion of Honor, the Walt Disney Family Museum and the Exploratorium, dot the city, displaying everything from the world's greatest fine art to wax figures of movie stars and famous characters from history.

Many communities and neighborhoods combine sports activities with a kaleidoscope of artistic classes and modes of expression, from dancing to painting. Teen and senior centers, community centers, recreation centers and country clubs provide opportunities for exercise, creative expression and camaraderie. Equestrian centers, golf courses, tennis courts, swimming pools, athletic fields, sports leagues, racquet clubs, skating rinks and lush parks combine with regional sites for hunting, fishing, hiking and camping. Residents and tourists alike enjoy the incredible natural areas in Muir Woods National Monument (Mill Valley), Golden Gate National Recreation Area (San Francisco), Tilden Regional Park (Berkeley/Orinda), and Mt. Diablo State Park (Clayton), among many others. Golden Gate Park, one of America's first urban retreats and one of the world's largest horticultural wonderlands, stretches from Stanyan Street to the majestic Pacific Ocean on 1,107 indescribably beautiful acres. Some of San Mateo County's fine state beaches are also perfect spots for whale watching, including Montara State Beach, Pillar Point Harbor and Half Moon Bay. If sailing is your passion, the San Francisco Bay enjoys a worldwide reputation for optimum conditions and sheer beauty.

Aficionados of shopping will find that the San Francisco Bay Area is a retail mecca of virtually endless treasures, from antique and specialty stores to art galleries and sprawling regional malls. The downtown international marketplace lures artists and activists to its kaleidoscope of merchandise, while sidewalk cafes and fine restaurants beckon the weary customer to relax and refresh. When the intrigue of San Francisco's cosmopolitan crowds begins to dim, you can explore the intimate neighborhood districts tucked away in San Mateo County's welcoming communities. For bargains and a collector's dream, look over the books, trinkets, and linens at one of the weekend flea markets or antique fairs.

Another magnet to the Bay Area is the abundance of professional sports thrills in the impressive arenas of San Francisco, Oakland and San Jose. Some of America's favorite teams clash with the competition, cheered on by frenzied fans. Imagine watching the SF Giants or Oakland A's play baseball, catching the action of the SF 49'ers or Oakland Raiders football teams, or cheering on the Golden State Warriors basketball team.

Day trips and weekend vacations are a common indulgence for Bay Area residents, who live within an easy drive from premier destinations like pristine Lake Tahoe and other alpine recreation areas, Pebble Beach and the Monterey Peninsula, and the award-winning wineries of the Sonoma and Napa Valleys. Where the San Francisco Bay meets the Sacramento and San Joaquin Rivers at the California Delta, more than 1,000 miles of sparkling waterways invite boating, fishing, camping, relaxing on a houseboat, water-skiing, jet-skiing, swimming and birding. The more adventurous may want to explore high-intensity sports like sky-diving, windsurfing, parasailing, canoeing, kayaking, white-water rafting, backpacking, bungee jumping and rock-climbing.

Award-winning public school districts are spread all across the Bay Area, providing students with exceptional preparation for an eventual university education. If you prefer the benefits of private school education, some top private schools include: Head-Royce School in Oakland, The Academy in Berkeley, St. Ignatius College Preparatory in San Francisco, College Preparatory School in Oakland, and Bentley School in Oakland/Lafayette. Certain Catholic schools in the area include Corpus Christi in Piedmont and St. Theresa and Bishop O'Dowd in Oakland. For those interested, the average tuition for a private high school in California is $15,617 and the average tuition for a private California elementary school is $9,650.

Finding the ideal home is easy in the San Francisco Bay Area, where spectacular waterfront properties, hillside retreats, and magnificent mansions mix with cozy bungalows or elegant Victorians. High-rise condominiums and luxurious townhouses with panoramic Bay views draw in the city's brilliant glow of lights, romance, and attractions. In the region's smaller communities, meticulous landscaping trimmed in greenery and blooms graces beautiful older homes along tree-shaded streets. Regardless of where you choose to settle in the Bay Area, you will find a gracious lifestyle that defies comparison. Little wonder that metropolitan San

Francisco glitters like a flawless diamond among metropolitan centers, intensely loved by those who are fortunate enough to call it home.

THE BAY AREA REAL ESTATE MARKET
San Francisco Housing Trends – An Overview

The crown jewel of the San Francisco Bay Area is of course the City by the Bay itself. With a real estate climate all its own, the city of San Francisco and its housing market merit a brief examination before we delve into the smaller housing communities to the East of the sparkling Bay.

With an estimated population of over 837,000 condensed within 47 square miles, San Francisco is classed as the fourteenth largest U.S. city. Thanks to its unparalleled setting and vigorous job market (along with the highest minimum wage in the country—$10.74—as of January 2014), San Francisco in recent years has become one of the most attractive—and most competitive—places to find a home. As such, the current housing market in the city proper is extraordinarily intense: competition is fierce among buyers and unprecedented numbers of homes are selling far above their asking prices. The rise in housing prices all over the city—including that of detached homes, condos, and apartments—indicates that there is much more demand for new housing than there is supply. The flock of new buyers rushing into San Francisco is a young and affluent crowd; many are first-time homebuyers and employees of the booming tech industry, which is based in the nearby Silicon Valley and in San Francisco itself. The city is becoming steadily denser, more affluent, and more expensive. The unfortunate result of this trend is that many longtime city residents are being forced out of their hometown, as rents continue to climb and the cost of living skyrockets.

In sum, if you are set on living within San Francisco itself, be prepared to pay above the asking price and to survive a bidding war in order to secure virtually any property you may find. As prices are expected to continue increasing in the coming months, now may be the best time to make your San Francisco housing purchase.

East Bay Area Market Trends – An Overview

Across the United States, home buyers and sellers are more savvy and insightful than ever before – both players expect more detailed information and more comprehensive assessments than were typically offered in the past. If you have made the decision to buy or sell real estate in the Bay Area, we want to help ensure that you can contend with the competition. In this increasingly educated real estate climate, it pays to know your local market so that you, too, can make informed decisions and achieve your housing goals.

The San Francisco Bay Area is currently favoring home sellers, making the current climate what is known as a **"seller's market"** (more about this in Chapter 2). It is an ideal time to be a home seller because there is a great deal of demand to move into the area, sales prices are climbing, and a shortage of inventory for sale means that buyers are forced to pay more than the asking price for a home. These conditions have combined to make the Bay Area one of the nation's hottest real estate markets this year. This is great news for those who want to sell their homes quickly: eager Bay Area buyers tend to close a deal in about a month, or even less. It is also worth noting that the sale of **luxury homes**—those selling for one million dollars or more—is on the rise in this area; improvements to the economy and a healthy rate of employment are making luxury living attainable for many Bay Area residents.

Another essential facet of the East Bay market that you must be aware of is its timing. All real estate markets are cyclical, and are more active at certain times of the year than at others. In the East Bay, the most competitive and active period for the housing market falls between

January and May 15th, when the greatest number of people is looking to buy. It is a common misconception in our area that the summer is the best time to place one's home on the market, but, in fact, the summer time is a slower period than the winter and spring. Here is why: in an affluent area such as the East Bay, many families use their summers to travel and take time away from home with their loved ones. Others may be busy with graduations, which can also require travel, and tend to occur in May and June. As such, much of the buyer pool is lost to vacations and family time during the summer months.

Because of the prevalence of summer vacations, July tends to be a better month for homebuyers than for sellers; there is less competition for homes in July when many other families are out of town. When August rolls around, the housing market becomes quiet across the board: school is starting, last-minute vacations are wrapping up, and busy families are getting back into the swing of their routines. Though real estate sales do begin to pick up in September and the fall months, it isn't until January, when the holiday season is at an end that the market truly picks up speed. Once January hits, people are returning to their regular schedules and work routines, and kids are back to school; thus buyers return to fulfilling their real estate needs. January and February are excellent months for a seller to bring his home onto the market. You may ask why, and this may seem contrary to what you envision. But, inventory is still low in January and February, and other sellers are just beginning the conversation about selling their homes in the spring. Limited inventory is ideal for a seller while competition is stiff for a buyer. Don't wait for the New Year to begin planning if selling is on the horizon. Having a strong grasp on the yearly timing of your local market will give you a leg up in choosing when it is the most profitable time for you to sell or to buy. Keep this timeline in the back of your mind as you ready yourself for your next big real estate move. Each market has a high selling season and a low selling season, so consult an agent in your specific area to find the time that's best for you as a buyer or a seller.

Whether you are looking to buy or to sell a home in the East Bay, it is essential that you have a firm understanding of the market in which you are doing business. The subsequent chapters in this guide—some targeted specifically for buyers, some targeted specifically for sellers, and others written for the benefit of all—will elucidate the ins and outs of real estate in this area, with helpful insights and tips designed to guarantee a successful home sale or a successful home purchase. To begin understanding the local market, let us proceed to a narrowing of focus as we hone in on the neighborhoods and communities that make up our precise corner of the East Bay.

East Bay Communities

Adam and I specialize in the following niche neighborhoods and communities, all tucked within the beautiful slopes to the east of the San Francisco Bay: Piedmont, Berkeley, and the Oakland Hills. While we have extensive real estate work experience throughout the East Bay, as well as in San Francisco itself, and although some agents will work further out, Adam and I prefer to concentrate our efforts on a modest number of towns and neighborhoods so as to provide the best, most comprehensive service to individuals moving in and out of those distinct markets.

If you are looking to buy or sell in other areas of the Bay Area—such as Orinda, Lafayette, Danville, San Francisco or Marin—we would be more than happy to refer you to experienced real estate professionals we trust in those areas. We pride ourselves on cultivating a strong referral network (read more about the importance of Referrals in Chapter 6), and would love to assist you in finding a specialist who works outside our own area of expertise.

If, however, you are interested in the Piedmont, Berkeley, or Oakland Hills markets, you have come to the right place. With over twenty years' experience in these specific markets—combined with the fact that

I was raised in Piedmont and we now raise our own family there—we could not feel more at home in the neighborhoods where we shop, work and play. When it comes to these particular East Bay communities, you will not find agents with more experience, dedication, or familiarity than we have. Below you will find the insider's perspective on these three key communities. It is our hope that an overview of each location will help you to identify which local area is right for you, should you be looking to relocate within the East Bay.

Piedmont

The City of Piedmont is a charter city of approximately 11,000 residents located in the beautiful Oakland Hills, overlooking the San Francisco Bay. The city, which is virtually built out, consists of established, high-quality, single-family homes on quiet, tree-lined streets. Piedmont is centrally located within a few minutes from Oakland and San Francisco on the West and Concord and Walnut Creek on the East. Within Piedmont's 1.7 square-mile area, there are five city parks and numerous landscaped areas which offer wooded paths, tennis courts, children's playgrounds and picnic facilities.

Families primarily move into Piedmont to take advantage of the outstanding and exclusive school district: students must live within the town of Piedmont to attend its first-rate schools. Piedmont's school system includes three elementary schools, one middle school, and one high school. Local families also value the small, close-knit atmosphere found in Piedmont. When people raise their children here, they decide to stay for its unparalleled sense of community and proximity to all of the Bay Area's gems. Among the neighborhoods featured in this description, Piedmont is the most expensive, followed by the Oakland neighborhoods of Crocker Highlands and Upper Rockridge.

Oakland

Oakland is a vibrant city comprised of many neighborhoods with various cultures, attractions and styles. Consider the following specific Oakland districts:

Crocker Highlands: Crocker Highlands is a charming neighborhood located in the Oakland Hills and situated between the lovely City of Piedmont, the quaint Glenview neighborhood, the bustling shops and restaurants on Lakeshore Avenue, and within close proximity to Highways 13 and 580. Crocker Highlands is comprised of mostly older, traditional homes built in the 1920s with a sprinkling of homes built in the '30s and '40s. Charming and gracious is how one might describe a typical Crocker Highlands home. It is a wonderful neighborhood filled with laughter and charm, sidewalks and trees. The community is very small and intimate, with no shops of its own. Each year, we are proud to support the Crocker Highlands Elementary School Auction and Home Tour. This public elementary school has become very popular due to an influx of affluent families moving into the neighborhood who are active participants in their children's education. After 5th grade, Crocker Highlands families may decide between nearby Catholic schools, private schools, or other schooling options for their children.

Glenview: "Rockridge East" is my personal description for Glenview, a community located just below Piedmont and Oakmore. The Glenview home is similar in style to the 1920s Rockridge craftsman bungalow, and is also situated in a bustling neighborhood featuring charming shops, cafes, a variety of restaurants and convenient services (including my favorite dog grooming shop and shoe repair). Though still suburban in nature, the charming community of Glenview provides more of an urban feel similar to that of San Francisco itself.

Oakmore & Beyond: Comparable to Montclair and Upper Rockridge and adjacent to Piedmont you will find predominately traditional homes in quaint neighborhoods, with sidewalks and small shopping districts to call their own. Oakmore is located across from the City of Piedmont, just off of Park Boulevard and Highway 13. Upper Oakmore belongs to the Montclair School District and attracts many families. This neighborhood tends to fall within the same price point as Montclair, Crocker Highlands, and Upper Rockridge. Lincoln Heights, Redwood Heights and the Laurel District are three additional popular neighborhoods just beyond the Oakmore District up Highway 13. These areas are especially suitable for starter homes and younger families just beginning to establish themselves.

Rockridge: Prior to the building of the Bay Bridge in 1936, Rockridge—located at the foot of the Oakland Hills between Alcatraz Avenue to the north and 51st Street to the south, and between Telegraph Avenue to the west and Broadway to the east—was a sleepy neighborhood of cottages and bungalows owned by those who preferred the quiet life to the urban bustle of San Francisco across the Bay. Today, many of these homes remain, and represent some of the most coveted real estate in the Bay Area, for several reasons: the weather in this particular microclimate is often sunny and warm; the commute from the Rockridge BART Station is easy; the homes on the leafy residential streets have been charmingly restored; and the area's main thoroughfare, College Avenue, is lined with atmospheric cafes, gourmet restaurants, independent bookstores and antiques shops that people go out of their way to patronize. While residents adore Rockridge for its mini urban environment and prevalent biking and walking opportunities, it is also true that the area is often congested and parking is difficult. Furthermore, rent prices are very high and are consistently climbing.

Upper Rockridge: Conveniently situated between the Montclair Village and College Avenue business districts, the Upper Rockridge neighborhood is nestled in the hills, with lovely vistas of the San Francisco Bay. Unlike Piedmont and Crocker Highlands for example, where 1920s homes are prevalent, Upper Rockridge is comprised mostly of post-fire, new construction homes located in the popular Hillcrest School District. This public school district continues through 8th grade and is accessible <u>only</u> to those homes that fall within district boundary lines. The neighborhood boasts some sidewalks, but they are not found across the board. With its slightly lower price bracket, many families feel that they get more for their money in Upper Rockridge than in Piedmont, for instance, where one will pay a higher price for a smaller home that is most likely in need of renovations. After the Oakland Hills fire, many larger homes were rebuilt (where the original home was much smaller) covering a significant portion of the lot, leaving a very small separation between neighbors. However, its proximity to shopping and business districts is an added bonus.

Montclair

Just off of Highway 13, tucked above the Montclair Village, Piedmont and Upper Rockridge in the Oakland Hills, this wooded retreat with mature trees boasts privacy and tranquility and is easily accessible to freeways, first-rate elementary schools and shopping. Montclair exhibits a more wooded and tree-filled environment than its neighboring towns, and is more spread out than Crocker Highlands and Piedmont. Consequently it is not as tight-knit a community. Montclair's neighborhoods offer a wide range of older and newer homes and a diversity of architectural styles. They do not, however, contain sidewalks, which can be difficult when raising families. Within Montclair you will find a wide range of price points, from affordable homes to higher-end homes. Much like those in the neighboring communities, many Montclair homes enjoy sweeping views of the Bay.

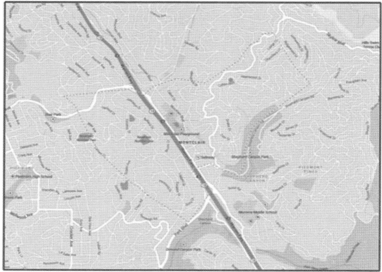

Berkeley

Sheltered by rolling hills and the San Francisco Bay, Berkeley is a vibrant and spirited city of unsurpassed richness. Within Berkeley's 18 square miles, a visitor can hear a symphony or a jazz quartet, stroll through a redwood forest or a rose garden, shop for Tibetan jewelry or for sportswear from The Gap, play a round of golf, take a yoga class, catch a world-premiere play or first-run film, embark on a sport fishing excursion or enjoy an architectural walking tour. Consummately Californian in its setting—but international in its cultural landscape—Berkeley is home to the University of California, Berkeley, which lends an academic air to the entire city. With its wealth of cultural and social diversity, dining and shopping opportunities and recreational pursuits, Berkeley is a compact city offering an exciting range of visitor options.

Families choose Berkeley for its wide selection of private schools and larger public school districts—Berkeley High School currently educates approximately 3,200 students—and unrivaled cultural opportunities, which are largely owing to the esteemed University that lends Berkeley its world-renowned status.

For those who are familiar with a large city environment, Berkeley will feel like home: there is something to do for everyone, and the city thus attracts every manner of people. Known as an urban, liberal university town, Berkeley prides itself on its charming older properties and stellar Bay views. Some homes in certain neighborhoods in Berkeley are far exceeding the high prices of some Piedmont homes.

CHAPTER 2: UNDERSTANDING THE HOUSING MARKET

Today's home buyers and sellers are savvier than ever. To persevere in this increasingly competitive, increasingly informed real estate environment, it is critical that you know your market. All **housing markets** are unique and different. In order to sell or to buy successfully, you must know the current market value of your house (for sellers), recognize what you can afford (for buyers), and familiarize yourself with the competition. Before setting housing goals for your future, take the time to assess your current, up-to-the-minute real estate market. Then determine whether or not your goals are in line with reality. This chapter outlines the key concepts you must grasp in order to be truly conscious of the state of your local housing market.

Is My Housing Market Hot, Cold, or Neutral?

HOT – Hot housing markets, also known as **seller's markets**, provide the best financial conditions in which to sell. They are characterized by the following factors:

❖ There are more interested buyers than there are houses available to buy.

❖ Sellers can sell their homes quickly, and for a higher price than they expected.

❖ **Bidding wars** often result in homes selling for prices greater than the **asking price**.

❖ Sellers are in the position of power to make negotiations and stipulations, since almost every available house is a hot commodity.

❖ In some cases a buyer will even waive certain buyer's rights (such as their appraisal, loan, and/or inspection contingencies – see Chapter 5 for more on

> *The ultra-hot East Bay real estate market is currently favoring home sellers. It's a great time to sell!*

Inspections, and Chapter 10 for detailed information on Contingencies).

COLD – Cold housing markets, also known as **buyer's markets**, provide the best financial conditions in which to buy. Cold markets can be identified by the following characteristic features:

❖ There are more homes available for sale than there are buyers to purchase them.
❖ Buyers are more likely to find the perfect home, since there are more homes from which to choose.
❖ Buyers themselves hold more of the power and influence, because there is more inventory and some sellers may be desperate to have their homes sold.
❖ Homes take longer to sell.
❖ Sellers are often more willing to negotiate, allowing buyers to buy for less than the asking price while including contingency periods in their offers for loan, appraisal, and home inspections.

NEUTRAL – Neutral housing markets are balanced markets. They are characterized by the following factors:

❖ The number of active buyers and sellers is relatively equalized.
❖ Homes' comparable sale prices are close to or equal to their active asking prices.
❖ Interest rates are more affordable.
❖ Houses sell within a normal time frame. The normal closing time for a typical sale is between 30 and 40 days.

What Are Comparable Sales?

One of the most accurate indicators of what a home is worth is the status of comparable homes sold in the area. For sellers, **comparable sales**, or comps, indicate what a fair asking price might be. Buyers utilize comps to determine whether or not the homes they are partial to are fairly priced. Comps should be linked to your home—or your dream home, if you're a buyer—based primarily on location and layout, the number of bedrooms and bathrooms, and loosely based on square footage. Other components, such as number of days on the market (or DOM); the asking price; parking arrangements; condition; quality of upgrades; proximity to schools, parks, shopping, and public transportation; the age of the home; yard capacity and access from the inside of the home to the back garden, may also be significant.

Virtually every competent real estate agent will offer to evaluate a seller's home against its comps in what is known as a **comparative market analysis**, or a CMA. These multiple-page reports will list several comps and their defining features, and will include a survey of active listings, pending listings, and sold listings that are categorically similar to the seller's home, as well as any comparable withdrawn or expired listings. Agents will perform a complementary CMA, as a way of advertising their competence and eagerness to earn the opportunity to work with you. Real estate agents have unique access to the most accurate Internet database of every home listed for sale, called the **Multiple Listing Service** (MLS). Agents utilize the valuable information on comps listed on this site to help their clients buy and sell homes.

If you have yet to begin working with a professional real estate agent, or should you wish to begin a comparative market analysis on your own, a great deal of information about local sold properties can be found online; many searchable databases exist, including the MLS—which you can find on most Realtor® websites, but will, however, provide only limited information—and those offered by many tax assessor's offices and county courthouses. For the County of Alameda, the Clerk-Recorder's Office provides a searchable online database of real property sales and transfers, which can be easily located by means of a simple Google search. Note: be wary of websites like Trulia, Zillow, and many others that may not provide an accurate indication of the value of a given home.

Why Do Home Prices Fluctuate? – Understanding Supply and Demand

Like many things in life, the housing market is in constant flux. Periods of boom (i.e. seller's markets) are closely followed by periods of bust (i.e. buyer's markets). The factors primarily responsible for regulating these boom and bust cycles are simple: **supply and demand**.

So what is it that drives the demand for—and therefore the price of—homes? **Demand** in the housing market is largely dependent upon the economic vitality of an area. Simply put, there is more demand for housing in places where reliable jobs are available. An ideal place to live is one where homes will appreciate well. In such a place, three elements will be present: 1) steady job growth, which encompasses active job creation and a decreasing unemployment rate; 2) job diversity, implying that employment options abound and the community does not chiefly rely on only one or two businesses for its success; 3) high job quality, or jobs that stem from growth industries, such as technology. A strong local economy—as is found in the Bay Area—increases sales activity, which is great news for home sellers. Homebuyers, however, often find themselves contending with steady price increases and bidding wars in such a lucrative economic atmosphere. Aside from consulting your real estate agent about the state of your local economy, you may choose to investigate the employment data kept by your local Chamber of Commerce or by the U.S. Bureau of Labor Statistics, which maintains records of current employment and wages by area and occupation.

How does the supply of housing affect home prices? **Supply** in this case refers to the amount of housing available, including both existing and new housing. When supply is low but the level of job creation is high, as is the case in the current Bay Area market, homes become more coveted and therefore more valuable. Another factor to consider in connection with housing supply is the supply of available land. Real estate prices have appreciated in the Bay Area over time in part thanks to the limited available supply of land on which to build new homes; San Francisco itself is surrounded by water on three sides, and much of the more rural suburban communities in the East Bay are either protected or already built up. Accordingly, the homes and rental properties that do exist are all the more valuable.

What Other Factors Affect Real Estate Pricing?

In addition to the demand for and supply of available housing, the **demographic composition** of an area will be a factor in the valuation of real estate and will determine what sorts of properties are available. The real estate market reflects the race, gender, income, and age of its constituents. For example, a community made up largely of homeowners from the "Baby Boom" generation will soon witness these individuals transitioning into retirement – this entails sizing down, moving into retirement communities, and potentially investing in vacation properties. Even advancements in healthcare can affect the real estate market: when the individual life expectancy increases, so will the demand for retirement homes to house ageing people.

Interest rates also play a major role in the fluctuation of home prices. When interest rates fall, the cost to obtain a **mortgage** goes down. If interest rates are lower, the cost of the loan is less and your actual monthly payment is less, making homeownership a more attractive option for buyers. Along with the increased demand for real estate comes an increase in home prices. The opposite occurs when interest rates augment. The cost of the loan will be higher, payments will be higher, and buyers will subsequently be able to afford less.

And, just as local economic activity affects the demand for housing in that area, the overall health of **the national economy** will influence real estate markets everywhere. Essentially, the strength of the economy and the strength of the real estate market go hand in hand: when the former is stagnant, so is the latter.

So What if I Want to Buy In Today's Seller's Market?

Though current real estate sales in the East Bay undoubtedly favor sellers, those looking to buy need not despair. If you are searching for your East Bay dream home, let the following tips help you to navigate a seemingly daunting seller's market:

- ❖ This is not the time to search for a "deal." Rather than hoping to pay less than a home is probably worth, make it your goal to pay **fair market value** for a home – whether that's <u>above</u> or below the asking price. Realize that your purchase is for the long term; your home will be a place where you and your family will reside and enjoy life for years to come.
- ❖ Consider searching for a property that requires a bit more TLC and fixing up. But be wary – only go for a fixer-upper if you're willing to invest the time and money necessary to bring the home up to your standards. Be realistic about the costs of fixing up a property. Ask yourself: will buying a fixer-upper really save me money in the end? Do I even have the time, the know-how, and the necessary resources to update a home? Will I be living in the home while I renovate or will I need to rent elsewhere, incurring additional out-of-pocket expenses?

- ❖ Look for a motivated seller. If your seller needs to sell his home fast and move on, he'll be more likely to sell it at or below market value. It pays to ask your agent to find out *why* sellers are selling.
- ❖ Don't disregard the time of year. More often than not, the winter months tend to be slower buying periods. This is certainly true of East Bay communities. It may, therefore, be beneficial to purchase

in the winter (between about November and December), when you will face a decrease in competition.

❖ Learn to be an effective communicator with your agent. If you aren't desperate to buy immediately, you are less likely to end up paying too much for a house that's not right for you. Not every house will be right for you. In a seller's market, you will, however, have to "reach" for a good house due to the competition. But, do know how to walk away from a sale if you feel a home is going to be too much work for you and/or for your budget. Your agent should support you in your decision. Do look at both sides of the coin. In an appreciating competitive marketplace, the question we ask our buyers is: what would it mean to you if you lost this home? We ask this when writing their offer, as we are trying to come up with their offer price. We ask the same question again if the inspections amount to higher than expected or unmanageable costs. Buyers need to be present at all inspections, read the disclosures thoroughly and ask questions. Buyers need to communicate their concerns and ask for clarity when needed. An agent cannot read minds but can help and guide those who ask and participate.

To Rent or to Buy –Which is Right for You?

If you are debating entering into the housing market, you may very well be a first-time homebuyer with experience renting. Many single people, couples, and families who have spent some years renting eventually reach a crossroads and find themselves asking the familiar question: is it better for me to continue renting or to purchase a home?

Both buying and renting come with their fair share of pros and cons. Like any major life decision, the choice to buy or to rent at a given time is one that merits considerable attention and careful reflection. Generally speaking, renting is wonderful for people who anticipate transition in the near future. For instance, if you are uncertain about your career path, are debating going back to school sometime soon, still want to explore many places before settling, or might decide to move to a new city or country in the foreseeable future, renting is your best bet. As a renter you have much more flexibility and freedom than you do as a homeowner. On the other side of the coin, buying is often preferable for those seeking to build a stable foundation and put down roots. If your career is established and secure, if you've selected a city or a neighborhood you want to live in permanently, and if you're prepared to stay there for at least five years, it probably makes sense for you to purchase real estate in the area you've chosen. However, this line of thinking merely provides a general guideline; to truly determine whether buying or selling makes most sense for you right now, you must take the time to evaluate certain financial and personal considerations.

Financial Factors

If you're weighing the options of buying versus renting, it goes without saying that you should first determine whether or not buying is a feasible option for you – in other words, whether or not you can afford to buy at this time. To find out if you can afford to buy, you will need to assess your ability to make a **down payment** (typically about 20% of the home's cost) and to pay the **closing costs** associated with the sale (about an additional 5% of the home's cost). Of course, these are just the initial costs involved in buying a home; when you buy you must also be able to afford to stay in the home. This involves a consideration of your long-term expenses, such as monthly mortgage payments, insurance, ongoing maintenance costs, and monthly debt payments.

A vast array of online calculators are available to help you factor in the various costs associated with both renting and buying. These calculators allow you to input values specific to your particular circumstances, and to weigh the two options for yourself. These online tools and their conclusions should never be trusted absolutely, however. In order to make their estimates, the calculators will ask you to predict a range of values (including the number of years you will stay in the home, the home's yearly rate of appreciation, and other factors you can't know for certain); their calculations, therefore, are only as accurate as the estimates you plug into them. Accordingly, take any calculated values with a grain of salt.

As a generic guideline for home buying, some financial experts suggest sticking to the "30-30-3 Rule." This rule dictates that, in order to be financially prepared to buy a home, you must have 30% of the home value saved up in cash, must spend no more than 30% of your monthly gross income on the mortgage, and pay no more than 3 times your annual gross salary for the home. Exceeding any one of these suggested rates can be risky, since you will also need to factor various maintenance costs into your monthly expenditures. This brings us to a major benefit of renting: maintenance and repair costs are already factored into one's monthly rent, and the landlord is responsible for conducting any repairs to the property. Therefore, renters are spared the headache (and the cost) of keeping up their home while homeowners must tend to and finance these matters on their own.

Even if you have determined that you can afford to make the initial purchase and cover the ongoing costs necessary to own a home, it is important to note that this does not necessarily mean it's best for you to buy. In other words, just because you *could* buy doesn't mean you *should* buy. Rather, you must decide whether or not buying a home will actually benefit you financially. In most cases in today's housing market, it will. As most readers are likely already aware, the long-term benefits of buying a house include the possibility of building equity, certain tax breaks, and the investment value of your home, which is likely to appreciate over time. For a more concrete financial analysis of your renting or buying options, we highly recommend the excellent online calculator developed and published by the New York Times' politics and policy website, The Upshot, titled "Is It Better to Rent or Buy?" The calculator allows users to adjust certain costs along a moveable scale, in order to evaluate their own specific situations and the cost of buying or renting over time. This exceptionally informative tool can be found online at www.NYTimes.com/interactive/2014/upshot/buy-rent-calculator.html, or by simply searching for the article title on an online search engine.

Once you know whether or not you can buy, as determined by your financial profile, the next step is to decide whether or not you should buy—a factor determined in large part by personal and emotional considerations. Indeed, the decision to rent or to buy is not just about finances – far from it! Where you live affects your state of happiness and well being, as well as your pocketbook.

Personal Factors

If someone were to tell you that you have to stay in your current residence for the next 10 years, how would you feel? Would you feel happy, merely OK or frustrated? If you know you would be happy to stay where you are for another decade, chances are you've found a wonderful place to live. This might mean that it's wise for you to consider settling there more permanently, and—assuming your finances permit you—to buy. If you have thoroughly examined all financial factors, now is the time to take your personal preferences and lifestyle plans into account.

No one but yourself and your family can decide these sorts of personal considerations, which can carry just as much weight in the decision-making process as the financial factors. It all comes down to determining which aspects of a dwelling place matter most to you.

When evaluating the choice to buy or to rent, you will need to weigh at least four major personal and emotional preferences:

1. **Home Environment** → Your decision to rent or to buy might also involve deciding between an urban or a suburban lifestyle. Be sure to weigh your preferences in terms of the housing environment. Do you love the hustle and bustle of the city? Do you participate in an active nightlife? Do you long for the privacy of the suburbs? How will your environment affect your daily commute to work? What sort of lifestyle will accompany your new living arrangement?

2. **Personal Flexibility** → Next, it is of the utmost importance that you assess the short- and long-term goals you have for your life. If you seek flexibility—i.e. if you intend to move abroad for a year, go back to school, or take a new job out of state any time soon—renting allows you the freedom to be mobile at relatively short notice. If necessary, you can always break a lease simply by writing a check. When you own a home, however, you have sacrificed flexibility for something that can be just as rewarding, depending on your lifestyle goals: stability. As a homeowner, you have made a more lasting commitment to a neighborhood and to a home. You have put down your roots in a community that you want to call your own. This means that you are much less mobile, though, should you decide

to pick up and leave. If you decide to move away after only a few years, you are likely to lose money and will have to navigate the sometimes-lengthy selling process before you can relocate.

3. **Capacity for Personalization** → When you buy a home, it becomes entirely your own. This means that every last detail is yours to customize according to your tastes. In picking the house, you choose the exterior architectural style you most prefer. After moving in, it is up to you to renovate, update, and personalize any feature of the home, inside or out. Homeowners often make changes to their yard and garden spaces, to their bathrooms and kitchen, and sometimes affix entirely new additions to the home itself. Homeowners are also free to make autonomous lifestyle choices when it comes to buying new pets or painting the walls, for example. When you rent, on the other hand, you are granted a much narrower degree of autonomy. While you can certainly personalize the interior furnishings of your rental property, you have no control over the exterior aesthetics (i.e. paint, roof, condition). Still, renters are spared the specific costs of maintaining, renovating, or repairing the property while homeowners must shoulder the burden of upkeep and repairs -- tasks that often cut into precious weekend time and scarce financial resources. Determine how much the ability to customize your home is worth to you.

4. **Emotional Satisfaction** → Lastly, you must find out what sort of residence will make you feel most content and fulfilled. If you're yearning for a sense of belonging, ownership, and stability, buying may be the right option for you. Homeowners get to enjoy the permanence of putting down roots, getting involved in a community, and raising a family in a place of their own. But perhaps you are most emotionally satisfied when you feel free and unsettled, with the ability to change the course of your life at a moment's notice. Or, perhaps you are simply looking for a place in which to sleep between

days at work and nights out with friends. You may simply prefer to have a landlord who handles all the maintenance and other worries for you. If any of these latter notions strike a chord with you, then you are likely to be happier renting.

The option you choose—renting or buying—is ultimately up to you and your pocketbook. If your finances are in order such that it would be financially beneficial to buy a home, the final outcome is reliant upon your personal preferences and emotional well being. Keep in mind that your decision is not a permanent one – if your position or opinions change later on down the road, your living situation may change too. Just because you can't afford to buy now doesn't mean you never will. On the other side of the coin, if you are happy renting, remind yourself that you don't have to buy a house now or ever. The decision of where to live is always yours to make, and should be dependent upon what makes you feel most comfortable and fulfilled.

As a quick and simple guide, we have provided the following table that outlines the Pros & Cons of both buying and renting. Consult this table for an abbreviated review of the points detailed above. We hope it will help you to visualize the choice between buying and renting a property.

Buying vs. Renting – The Pros and Cons

	Pros	Cons
Buying	• Sense of stability and permanence • A place to call your own • Connection to community • Financial incentives and significant tax benefits • Ability to personalize • Perfect if you're ready to stay put (you love your location and your job, your family size is relatively fixed, etc.)	• More responsibility (i.e. repairs and upkeep) • Much more time-consuming • Initially more expensive (in most cases) • Costs of moving in and out • Less mobility and flexibility, harder to move or to change your plans
Renting	• Landlord deals with repairs and upkeep • Less responsibility = more free time • Smaller monthly expenses (in most cases) = ability to conserve cash • Lots of flexibility – you are able to pick up and leave • Perfect if you anticipate change (i.e. a new job, a new baby, another degree, etc.)	• Much less ability to customize and personalize your space • Restrictions on your lifestyle (i.e. ability to have pets, make noise, paint walls, remodel, etc.) • Less autonomy – you are somewhat at the landlord's mercy • Less feelings of stability or belonging – No investment

CHAPTER 3: Myth Busting – Addressing Common Misconceptions

Residential real estate markets are extremely localized – they are distinct everywhere you go. Each market behaves in its own unique way, in its own timing, and each real estate agent has his or her own individual method of doing business. Therefore, when it comes to real estate, it can be very dangerous to extrapolate or buy into any commonplace assumptions.

Real estate myths, expectations, hunches, and theories abound, and, with the disseminating power of the Internet, it is easier than ever for the average buyer or seller to place confidence in generalized claims that may or may not be true. Therefore, we have created a list of common misconceptions, applicable to both buyers and sellers, which we hope to disprove or to clarify in the context of our particular East Bay markets. Each numbered myth or theory—identified in quotation marks—is analyzed in a paragraph below.

Keep in mind that it is of the utmost importance that you feel well informed and knowledgeable about all of the key variables associated with buying or selling a property. Don't let pre-conceptions (often incorrect) about your market cloud your judgment. You don't want to find out at the closing table that you were unaware of how closing fees, applicable local taxes, prorated property taxes, etc. are allocated at the closing.

Should you ever come across an additional real estate myth or assumption, different from those listed below, feel free to contact Adam or myself, or another agent you trust, to discuss whether or not the myth rings true in reality.

Common Misconceptions for Buyers

1. "Buying and owning is always preferable to renting."

While the common assumption is that buying is somehow superior to or at least preferable to renting, homeownership is not for everyone. Both buying and renting have different advantages for those in different stages of life. Renting is a terrific option for anyone who may be moving again in the near future, while buying is preferable for those who intend to stay put for five years or more. Many people choose to rent when the size of their family may be about to change, or if they face the possibility of re-locating for work. Home buying, on the other hand, tends to suit families in more stable, permanent situations. Additionally, renting can be a better choice for those who either cannot or do not wish to commit to a great deal of upkeep or responsibility; homeownership requires near constant maintenance, since there is no landlord to maintain your property for you.

For those individuals or families who are in a more stable phase of life, however, buying a home can have many diverse and lasting advantages. For instance, most people living in affluent communities, such as those found in the East Bay, can take advantage of the tax breaks that are associated with home ownership. Plus, owning a home allows people to feel that they have a place of their own and a comfortable sanctuary in which to raise their families and build a life.

In short, it is ultimately up to you to decide whether buying or selling is preferable for you at this stage in your journey. If homeownership isn't most suitable to your current lifestyle, that doesn't mean it won't become a viable option in the future. When it comes to choosing a residence, it is most important to evaluate your own lifestyle and plans for the near future, rather than to rely on the opinions of others.

2. "Buying costs more than renting."

This myth is a dangerous one because it can discourage many people from buying when doing so might actually be a wise financial move for them. The notion that buying is always more expensive than renting is a blanket statement, one that makes sweeping generalizations and is therefore not always reliable. While the ticket price on a home for sale will always be greater than the price for a rental property, this only indicates that buying typically costs more at the outset. What many people fail to grasp is that buying generally increases your net worth over time. If you calculate how much your monthly rent would add up to over the course of five years, it just may be that purchasing a home is a more cost-effective choice in the long run—especially when you factor in the many tax breaks that homeowners receive, which most people need and which will immediately begin to pay off.

3. "Real estate agents require large commissions."

If as a homebuyer you are wary of hiring a buyer's agent due to a concern about cost, you are sorely (and happily!) mistaken. There are virtually no costs to you as a buyer in utilizing an agent – in fact, it is customary in the East Bay (as it is in most markets) that the seller pays the commission of both the seller's and the buyer's agent. These commissions come out of the proceeds of the sale, and not out of the buyer's pocket.

One thing many people don't realize is this: Realtors® do not get paid a single penny until a transaction closes. This means that, if an agent makes an offer to buy a house on behalf of her client and that offer is rejected in favor of another, that agent does not get paid for all the work she has done for her client up until that point. In a hot market like the current one, people assume that agents make great sums of money—but not every client gets the house he or she makes an offer on. In any given real estate transaction, there is only one buyer who comes out victorious; if that person is not you, your agent will not be compensated for all her efforts on your behalf. A buyer's agent understands just how difficult and time-consuming the home buying process can be and so seeks to inspire buyers, keeping them energized and optimistic that the right house will come along. As I write this passage, this exact scenario happened to the clients with whom I met today. These clients eventually succeeded, finally prevailing in their third multiple-offer situation, having lost two homes to multiple offers prior to this big win. Just as I tell all my clients, the home you end up buying after a few losses always works out to be a better home than the rest. For some reason, this is just the way it always happens. In the end, if a buyer gives up, as some do, and doesn't close on a home, the agent is not paid at all. It happens more often than one might think.

Cost-free or costly? There are no drawbacks to working with buyer's agents. Since this is what they do, day in and day out, they are there to make the process smoother, calmer, and more straightforward for you. Plus, their services are virtually cost-free – clearly one of the major benefits of buyer representation. If, on the other hand, buyers attempt to represent themselves the issues that arise can be costly.

4. "If you're in love with a home, you should always go way over budget to secure it."

Some people will tell buyers—especially first-time home buyers—that, once you find the dream home, it is worth it to spend nearly all your money to obtain that home. While it's true that buying a house will deplete much of your earnings and savings—indeed, it is likely the largest single investment you will ever make—still, it is important to make financial decisions that are sustainable for the long haul. If you do decide to put down the big bucks in order to win the bidding war on the home of your dreams, first be sure that you will be able to sustain the higher mortgage payments over the course of many years. Speak with your agent and lender to determine what you can afford before your heart prompts you to make a hasty decision.

5. "The house itself is the single most important deciding factor in a purchase."

Of course it is true that the home itself is a major consideration—after all, the house is your investment and represents your most valuable piece of property. This home must provide you and your family with a lasting and authentic source of comfort, happiness, and security. Still, in light of all the demands placed on your new dwelling, it can sometimes be easy to neglect the other factors one must bear in mind—factors that are of near equal importance to the home itself.

Firstly, location is everything. Your home may be lovely, but how is the neighborhood? Is it loud, overcrowded, or unsafe at night? Next consider proximity – how close are you to your workplace, or to the nearest grocery store, shopping center, elementary school, or highway? Even when first buying a home, it is never too early to consider resale. What are the development plans for the neighborhood in the next several years? It pays to know the local economy and the local people before you move in.

Also consider the land your home is built on. Is there a yard? Is it on an up-slope, on a down-slope, or (ideally) level? The yard is important for **resale value**, and may become more important to you if your family expands or if you choose to buy a new pet, for example. Does the yard come equipped with a swimming pool? While pools undoubtedly provide hours of enjoyment, keep in mind that they can also be seen as a liability issue and may therefore detract from the property's value when your time to sell the home rolls around.

And, of course, price is always a factor. Any given buyer should only pay what he or she can afford, no matter how ideal the house may seem. When taking a moment—or several—to think over the value of your property, community, local economy and neighborhood, make sure that the combined value of all these various components does indeed add up to the price you will be paying for the home.

All of these factors and more can be just as significant as the look and feel of the house itself. Don't make the mistake of falling head over heels for a house—which is just a building after all—unless the other elements of long-term success and happiness match up as well.

Common Misconceptions for Sellers

1. **"I don't need a seller's agent. I am perfectly capable of performing a For Sale By Owner (FSBO)."**

    Some sellers argue that listing agents and their services are over-rated. They may therefore decide to attempt what is called a **For Sale By Owner** (or FSBO) – in other words, they may try to sell their home by themselves without the assistance of a **seller's agent**. FSBO is in no way encouraged, under any circumstances. On many occasions, we have experienced firsthand the negative end results of an attempted FSBO. The reasons to avoid FSBO are almost innumerable. Before accepting the myth that FSBO is a viable option, consider the following disincentives:

    Firstly, if you want to have a professional job done, you must hire a professional. If, for example, you ever required surgery, you wouldn't perform it on yourself, or diagnose yourself, if you were a doctor – you would trust a specialist. In the same way, you will be doing yourself a disservice if you attempt to sell a home on your own, without professional guidance. Without a fulltime agent's negotiation skills, for instance, you will almost certainly end up under-selling your home or leaving money on the table. Without an agent's insider knowledge of your local market, you won't be able to pick up on the unique idiosyncrasies of your area. If you aren't aware of market trends, your sale will not turn out well.

    Secondly, without the agent's knowledge and connections, you won't have access to required contracts, disclosures, and other paperwork. The average person only buys two or three homes in a lifetime, and is therefore relatively unfamiliar with the process of dealing in real estate. Unless you are already a real estate guru, you most likely do not have extensive experience in handling the complex paperwork associated with selling and buying property. If you overlook certain documentation, you risk being sued. In addition, on your own you will not have any working relationships with local service providers, nor will you have the expertise required to deal with their reports when they come in. When there is an agent representing and supporting you, you are protected from certain service providers' attempts to take advantage of homeowners; without an agent, you are entirely on your own.

An agent's many jobs will all be placed on your shoulders if you choose to work independently. Ask yourself if you have the time, skills, and resources to market and publicize your home all on your own. The important task of marketing your property is no small consideration. If you don't know how or where to best advertise your home, you will be at a severe disadvantage as compared to other represented sellers. Plus, without an agent you will not have full access to the Multiple Listing Service (MLS), the most effective platform for marketing your property to buyer's agents and their clients.

Then, keep in mind that the process of selling a home is always very emotional. Even with a Realtor®'s help, it is hard for sellers to make unbiased judgments. If you are working on your own, it will be even harder – there will be no one there to temper your partiality or to give you a neutral perspective on other comparable home values. Without these objective insights, you will have a very difficult time selling your home successfully.

Furthermore, as a seller, it is likely that you have a career of your own. Unless real estate is your full-time job, you won't have the time to devote yourself to this endeavor 24/7, as an agent would. In the real estate world there is no time to say "I'll get back to you tomorrow" because of career or family commitments – there are constant deadlines that must be met. And because real estate is not what you do professionally, you also will not be connected to the wider community of other agents. If you are one person working on your own, your network is exceedingly narrow.

Even if you do manage to secure an interested buyer, the buyer's agent (if he or she has one) will be reluctant to work with you. The agent may even recommend against the purchase when speaking with the client. This is because the buyer's agent will, understandably, wonder why you are working on your own. He or she will question the condition of the home if the seller can't even afford to hire a professional to sell it. Many agents will skip right over your home since they will be wary of the product you are offering. A FSBO raises red flags, in the same way that hiring an out-of-area real estate agent or company does (for more on Red Flags, see Chapter 9). Not to mention that agents realize that, in a FSBO, the seller has no real knowledge of what they are doing. Constant changes, updates to disclosures, and adjustments to industry protocol occur so frequently that it will be impossible to keep up if you aren't a full-time agent. Moreover, if a buyer does engage in an offer with a FSBO, the buyer's agent will inevitably end up representing both buyer and seller by default, as the agent is the most knowledgeable one in the group. This is unfair and ill-advised, since no agent wants to be liable for someone they do not know, let alone someone who is looking for a deal; the situation has "lawsuit" written all over it. If you are trying to sell your home in the most successful manner possible, it simply is not in your best interest to give off these negative impressions, both to prospective buyers and to their agents.

Ultimately, if you do attempt a FSBO, it is likely that your plan will fall through anyway, since another agent (either a buyer's or seller's) will end up needing to get involved to assist in closing the deal. This frequently happens, since sellers realize after a few weeks that they alone cannot handle the many tasks performed by a seller's agent. If the FSBO had hired an agent in the first place, he or she would have achieved a better profit and a more seamless transaction. So rather than dealing with the added stress, it is vital that all sellers, under any circumstances, work with a professional agent.

In sum, if you attempt a FSBO, agents and potential buyers may be wary of the product you are offering, its condition and presentation;

not to mention, emotions will run high. In turn, issues and lawsuits are inevitable. It's just too risky, financially and emotionally. It all comes down to this: if you want your home to sell in a smooth and advantageous manner, you must rely on the skills of a specialist – just as you would with a doctor, surgeon, financial advisor, or lawyer.

2. "Seller's agents charge steep commissions."

If money is your concern, you may be surprised to learn that you will not pay your agent a single cent until your deal has closed and your house is sold. It is the norm for sellers to pay the commissions of both agents involved in the transaction—the buyer's and the seller's agent. A typical commission is 5 or 6% of the sale, split 50/50 between both agents (i.e. 2.5 or 3% per agent). The agent also has to give his or her company a cut of each commission, as applicable. However, these commissions come out of the proceeds you will make from the sale of your home, not from funds or savings you previously held. Also, if you change your mind or if your transaction for some reason falls through, your agent won't be paid at all. An agent might spend a year's time working with you, but if your buyer decides to stay in their current home or decides to buy elsewhere, your agent ends up working for free and makes nothing (a commission is earned only after the agent has secured a committed buyer). Sometimes, if sellers are unable to sell for their ideal price they too will choose not to sell at all, and their agent will not get paid. In certain

situations, agents can end up spending hours and hours of their time working for free. Seller's agents, like buyer's agents, only receive their commissions when they succeed in selling a home and closing the deal.

Furthermore, once you take a moment to appreciate all the work a seller's agent does for you—from advertising and marketing, to coordinating and orchestrating—you will understand that real estate agents run an entire business of their own, and the compensation they receive for their efforts is commensurate with the time, knowledge, skills, and experience they put into each sale. If an agent's commission seems steep to you, keep in mind that all of the advertising costs spent to attract buyers to your home come out of your agent's own pockets. Your agent is an independent contractor and not an employee; she has to keep her business running like any other business owner. Agents must pay errors and omissions insurance, and their own health and car insurance, to name a few of the larger out-of-pocket expenses; along with the many costs associated with being a Realtor®, the list is endless. Agents do not receive a draw or a salary, but work solely on commission.

Many clients are surprised by our above-and-beyond approach, especially after countless hours and multiple phone conversations with our clients at all hours of the day and night – we do those "extra" things simply because we are good, passionate, caring, and considerate agents. From what I have learned from speaking with our clients over the years, most other agents seek to do the bare minimum, and this truly surprises me. Adam and I could not imagine doing less or taking care of our clients any less thoroughly than we do! You may wonder why. I think the reason is that we both not only love what we do, but place ourselves in the shoes of our buyers and sellers each and every time. I think this is what truly makes the DiMaggio/Betta Difference.

3. **"Any renovations or remodels that my home needs can be left to the new homeowners."**

When you are preparing to sell your house, especially if you are striving to sell your home in a hurry, it can be tempting to leave any minor updates or renovations to the new buyers who are soon to move in. While it's true that you shouldn't go completely overboard with exorbitant remodels (they may cost more to complete than the value they will add to your property), certain pivotal improvements might just make the difference in selling your home quickly and above the asking price. Basic updates to key areas like the flooring, kitchen appliances, landscaping, and painting can help move your home into a higher price bracket. Also, it's valuable to consider the point of view of your buyer – your buyer is hoping to move into a home that is ready to be lived in. If you throw a long list of necessary renovations at him or her, a buyer will be less enthusiastic about your home and, in turn, you will not have as many buyers making offers on your home. You then lose the momentum necessary for a multiple-bid, over-asking experience. You get only one chance to make a good impression – there are no second chances, so be sure to listen to your agent and do it right the first time. To entice a buyer who will love your home as much as you do, take the time and effort to present your home in its most appealing light.

To prepare your home for market, your agent will bring in a team of trusted service providers to give estimates as to what certain basic updates and renovations might cost. After receiving these bids, sit down with your agent and prioritize. Decide which of these jobs are mandatory and what makes financial sense for you. It is more important now than ever to do everything you can to present a beautiful home. Depending on the amount of work to be done, your home renovations can be completed within about 10 days to 3 weeks.

4. "Holding too many open houses will make me appear overly desperate to sell my home."

Some agents or fellow home sellers may warn you that holding multiple **open houses** in the course of a few weeks can make you appear desperate. You may worry that potential buyers will think there is something wrong with your home if it is still held open after an extended period of time. While market conditions may result in differences elsewhere, in the local East Bay market it is beneficial to leave a home open until it sells. Because new buyers are coming into town every day, it doesn't make sense to close a home before the right people have viewed it and until a serious offer (or offers) has been made. If people are not given access to a property, readily and easily, there is less chance for an offer. Also, a home needs to be left accessible to those buyers who do their

house hunting on the Internet – they may spot your home online and be intrigued by the photographs, but decide they need to see the property in person. No buyer can truly get a feel for a home based on what he or she sees online; to be able to judge the property, its layout, and its specific location accurately, a buyer must actually walk through it. If your house is no longer open, you have excluded these potential buyers. You might ask: why don't these buyers contact an agent? Oftentimes they will not contact an agent because they think they aren't really ready to purchase, they don't want to bother an agent, or they don't have the time. Instead, they simply choose to put that particular house on the backburner, and the seller loses out. Over the years we have sold homes that buyers previewed during our open houses. These homes had all been on the market for some time. In two of the instances, the buyers were not even looking to buy but found that the particular home just struck a chord with them. Sellers, a word of advice – *don't shortchange yourselves.*

We always choose to keep a listed home open until it has sold. In our experience, many clients' sales were made simply because a home was open – in some cases the buyer turns out to be the person who didn't think he was looking to move, but stopped by an open house and fell in love with the property. It is in fact common for a home to sell to someone who wasn't even looking to buy, as noted above. For this reason alone, open houses are a great way to attract attention, foot traffic, and buyers! If you truly wish to sell your house, you have to allow people to see it.

5. "If we set our home price high, we can always negotiate down."

An inexperienced or dishonest seller's agent may try to persuade you that your home is worth more than it is, and advise you to set a higher asking price than you can realistically expect to earn when the home sells. This is referred to as "buying a listing," and is very dangerous advice. First off, pricing too high will immediately eliminate a portion of potentially interested buyers who find your steep price to be outside of the realistic price range. It is always best to set a realistic asking price, based on comparable sales. If you do so, you may be able to generate some enthusiasm and competition, which may in turn lead buyers to bid up! If you or your agent chooses an asking price that is too high to begin with, however, this option is unlikely to be open to you.

When a price is set too high a buyer will not make an offer. Buyers will not wish to insult you by offering something lower. Thus, buyers will instead choose to wait around until you eventually lower your price, or will go find another home. You as the seller will begin to wonder why no offers are being made on your property, whether at or below the price you have asked for, and this will be the reason. Rather than offend you, buyers wait for your price to eventually come down after a couple of weeks, and then begin to make their offers. This is a rather common practice in our area, and one that your agent has no control over. To avoid this unfortunate scenario, always opt to set a fair and practical asking price from the get-go.

6. "After receiving an offer, wait a while before responding to the buyer."

This is the sort of advice that should make you run quickly in the other direction! As a seller, it is imperative to remember that every offer merits attention and respect. When you receive an offer to buy your home—regardless of whether you feel it meets your high expectations for your sale—it is your duty to respond in a timely and professional manner. Every offer to purchase a home is made by a real live human being who is seriously interested in purchasing your house from you. No offer is a joke, and no potential buyer deserves to have his or her feelings jeopardized in some sort of waiting game. Prior to the offer date, typically a week to ten days before they can make an offer on your home, the buyers have spent hours and hours thinking about your home, reading over disclosures, asking questions, holding long conversations with their agent and with service providers (and possibly with friends and family members as well), and have maybe even paid for pre-inspections on a home they don't yet own. To make a buyer who has so much invested in your home wait around to hear back from you is not a good idea. Emotions are running high.

Waiting around to respond to a buyer's offer can only hurt you – in doing so, you risk losing the opportunity to make a sale. Instead, respond right away and begin the process of negotiating, if necessary, and closing the deal if it is the right fit (see more on the Offers process in Chapter 10).

When we work with sellers, Adam and I treat every offer with the utmost consideration. When we hear offers from potential buyers, we instruct our sellers to make a decision so that we can contact the buyer's agent *that same day*. This is done out of respect for the potential buyers, who have spent countless hours pondering over your home. Also, these buyers may need to act quickly and make an offer the following day on another house if you reject them. Or, on the other hand, they may experience buyer's remorse and actually pull their offer to buy your home. If you make them wait too long, another home may come onto the market that appeals to them more.

In sum, treat all offers as you would want any offer of your own to be treated – with serious consideration and careful thought. Respond promptly so as to set a punctual precedent. (Note: Buyers should show the same consideration to sellers as well. As soon as buyers have finished their home inspection(s) and are satisfied, they should remove the contingency right away rather than waiting for the full term of their contingency period to expire. Here, again, is another way to set the tone for a successful sale.)

7. **"A negotiation is successful only if you receive all your stipulated terms."**

This myth is another perilous blanket statement. Any negotiation—whether in the real estate realm or otherwise—is ultimately about compromise. Keep this in mind when reading over offers from potential buyers. In the same way that your home will likely not have every single feature that your buyer hoped for in a dream property, it is unlikely that you will receive each one of your desired terms. A successful real estate negotiation involves both parties coming to a mutually satisfactory agreement – one that makes both sides feel comfortable and gratified.

Sometimes it is the agents themselves who need to keep this in mind; some agents get angry or uptight when things don't go exactly as they hoped they would. <u>But all agents should remember that they are facilitators, and not competitors</u>. An agent's job is to represent his or her clients and make the process as smooth as possible for them; it is not about the agent or his or her own ego. As such, we strive to reach mutually acceptable terms in every transaction. We are neutral and simply relay the information back and forth. I must say, Adam is the most patient person I know; he rarely, if ever, allows his emotions or personal opinions to interfere. Though we work well with our colleagues, not all agents do. This is why it is so important, from the very beginning, to choose an agent who is a team player and a collaborator, not a winner-take-all competitor. For any agent's long-term success, he or she should cultivate relationships with other agents in the real estate community, not alienate them. We should all work as a team, rather than as individual islands. If one agent has the listing, another is going to bring the buyer; that's just how it works, so it pays to be kind.

General Myths for Both Buyers & Sellers

1. **"It isn't necessary to work with either a buyer's or a seller's real estate professional."**

    Some friends or family members may try to tell you that it is easy enough to work in real estate on one's own, and that you therefore don't need to bother with hiring an agent. This is a huge mistake. It is more than worth it to have an experienced professional on your team, one who knows the market inside and out and can do the tedious and demanding background work for you, while you continue on with your normal life and continue working.

    If you think you can fulfill the role of an agent on your own, consider the many difficulties involved in a real estate transaction. First, the real estate market is full of legal and professional jargon, complex documentation, ongoing changes, and stiff competition. Buying or selling a house is sure to be the biggest—and most stressful—financial move you will ever make. In addition, settling your family in a new place is confusing and time-consuming. It can be frustrating to keep on top of constantly changing laws and documentation, since home-buying and -selling customs vary in different parts of the country. Therefore, even if you knew how to navigate the real estate market in your old hometown, you may be out of your element in your new one. For example, someone moving to the East Bay from a newer housing development out of state may not understand the purpose of the many home inspections we typically carry out here, and may not know how to decipher them. But when you're buying an older, 1920s-era home in Piedmont or Crocker Highlands, for example, the home buying process is much more complex.

Professional real estate agents exist to guide you smoothly through the entire process in your new market. Agents demystify confusing processes and jargon, and provide the information and **disclosures** that outline everything you need to know about a given house and, more importantly, notify you when a disclosure has been left out! Especially in today's fast-paced, intense market climate, having a team of professionals on your side is critical. Agents come equipped with a ready-made cohort of inspectors, mortgage lenders, stagers, escrow/title companies, and repairmen whom they trust. Without an agent to manage all of these various professionals, you would be left on your own to track down a team who may or may not have experience in your area or a solid reputation. Lastly, stellar agents know their markets intimately. They keep abreast of day-to-day market trends in a way that a website or a news report cannot. Only an agent will be able to accurately read the current market and advise you accordingly – whether it relates to the best time to buy or sell, the fairest price for your home, or the best neighborhood for what you can afford.

To conclude, there is no real replacement for a full-time, professional, successful real estate agent at the top of his or her game. Therefore, talk to an agent before you begin the process of buying or selling on your own! Education is key and it is never too early to begin speaking with an agent. It's not a waste of time; it's a process, and something that takes time for a buyer or seller to digest and understand. There is nothing to lose in beginning the conversation, and determining for yourself what a given agent has to offer you. We also advise buyers and sellers alike to avoid the urge to read up on real estate trends in the many generalized self-help guides on the market – these guides do not apply fully (if at all) to our specific **micro-market** here in the East Bay. Indeed, that's why we're writing this book!

2. "Resources and tools on the Internet will serve me just as well as a real estate agent would."

It's certainly true that online resources are extremely useful. They can provide you with great background information, a basic understanding of what properties are out there, and what these properties sold for in your market. These tools can't, however, replace a living, breathing professional whose job it is to help you maximize your individual goals, and who is keenly aware of market conditions as they are occurring – and not a month later.

When surfing the web for real estate information, bear in mind that much of what is published online or broadcast on the news may not be relevant to our local micro-market. Each market is unique, and sweeping generalizations only conflict the buyer, as well as the seller. Current housing trends in New York or L.A. are not relevant here. Indeed, as the first chapter of this book makes apparent, even San Francisco's real estate market is distinct from those immediately to the east of it. To understand the nuances that distinguish your particular market, you will need the help of a local agent rather than a nationwide or regional website.

Moreover, though the Internet contains a wealth of information for buyers and sellers, there are several online search engines accessible only to Realtors®. The most beneficial online real estate database, the MLS, is one of these that provide specialized access solely to real estate professionals. Consequently, it is in the best interest of any buyer or seller to use the two resources—the Internet and an agent—in conjunction. Your agent will in fact be able to recommend trusted, local websites for you to consult.

CHAPTER 4:
ALL ABOUT BUYING

The decision to buy a house is likely to be simultaneously one of the most exhilarating and most intimidating experiences of your life. Especially for first-time homebuyers, the extensive process involved in the purchase of a home can seem incredibly daunting. Because the average person tends to buy only two or three homes in a lifetime, most people do not have extensive home buying experience and therefore need time to become familiar with the procedure and the jargon.

Now that you have decided the time is right for you to buy a home, it's up to you to do a fair amount of homework at the outset, to ensure that you're as informed as you can be about your decision and its consequences. With the profusion of resources available on the Internet, there is no reason for you to be any less prepared than the other buyers on the market. Then, once you have obtained a dependable real estate agent, you will have access to a constant source of assistance, motivation, and encouragement. With your agent's additional expertise, the prospect of buying a new home will begin to appear not only doable, but also practical.

Indeed, owning a home comes with numerous financial and tax-related benefits, as well as social benefits to the family, to children, and to the community. When you own a home you achieve a sense of permanence and belonging in your community. Besides providing you and your family with a place to call your own, owning a home should help you to accomplish your financial goals. Think of it this way: you're always going to need a place to live and, in the long term, inflation is all but guaranteed. Therefore, even if buying a home seems a bit of an obstacle today, in some years down the road you will be happy you did so. Congratulations on your decision to become a new homeowner! Take to heart the ensuing advice and recommendations.

Choosing the Buyer's Agent

The **buyer's agent**, also known as the selling agent, is the professional real estate agent whose job it is to assist you in finding and then settling into your new home. This involves helping you locate the perfect property, advising you as to how much that home is worth, and negotiating for that home on your behalf. Though you yourself are in control of your home-buying experience, your agent will be your second-in-command and the person on whom you rely for guidance and wisdom. As such, it is imperative that you select your buyer's agent with care, seeking out a professional, fully qualified and personable worker.

As any experienced agent will tell you, <u>it is never too early to educate yourself on your local housing market</u>. Even if you are not intending to buy a home for another year or more, it is mutually beneficial to both you and your future agent to begin working together early on. No successful agent will consider it a burden to be contacted for preliminary information and advice; in helping you to understand your market before you're ready to actually look for a home, the agent ensures that you are well prepared when the time comes. If you begin the conversation in advance, you'll be prepared to take action by the time you are ready. Like an athlete preparing for a grueling competition, a savvy homebuyer must do some warming up before jumping into the game.

Regardless of where you are in your decision to purchase a home, any agent you work with must be at the top of his or her game. Here's how to identify an agent worthy of your business.

Before you Begin Looking – Even before you begin your search for a stellar agent, consider these pointers.

❖ **You do in fact need an agent.** There is no reason for any buyer to work without a buyer's agent. For one thing, it is common practice that the seller pays the commissions of both agents involved in a sale – meaning that the agent's services are virtually free for the buyer himself. Furthermore, no one but a professional will have the insights you need to make this critical financial decision and to help you carry out an optimal purchase. While the Internet is full of useful resources, no website can replace personal experience and knowledge. When you have specific questions about reports, disclosures, or your particular market, community and neighborhood, you won't find all the answers online.

❖ **Be aware of what you are looking for.** Before you interview local agents or ask for referrals from friends and family, make a mental checklist of what it is you want out of this partnership. For example, if you're looking for a personal, one-on-one relationship, you probably won't be happy working with an agent who employs an extensive staff of assistants. If you know what you're looking for before you begin looking, you have a greater chance of finding the right match.

❖ **Be prepared to interview prospective agents.** Expect to interview two or three prospective agents, since this is likely to be the biggest financial decision of your life and you want an experienced professional to represent you. Plus, you will be spending a great deal of time with your agent – it is important that you get along with him or her and genuinely like his or her working style.

❖ **Understand what your agent will—and won't—do.** Be aware from the outset that your agent's job will be to advise and to facilitate, to provide the necessary contextual information you need, and to advocate for you. His or her job will not be to make major decisions for you or to come up with an offer price on a home for you – you are the decision maker since the home you choose is your investment.

The Selection Process – These tips will assist you in narrowing your search and honing in on the perfect agent.

❖ **Seek advice from friends you trust. Referrals** are exceedingly helpful in this industry. Ask friends, family, coworkers, and anyone you come into contact with in your new neighborhood—a cashier, a schoolteacher, a parent—what it is they like about their community, and if they can recommend a professional and reputable local Realtor®.

❖ **Steer clear of online search engines.** Websites such as www.RealEstateAgent.com, www.AgentHarvest.com, and www.NeighborCity.com provide searchable databases of agents in many markets. However, these online tools are paid sources, and do not highlight all qualified candidates. Such sites cannot replace a person and should not be trusted over a personal referral. Do some general online research of your own to determine which local agents seem to have the best online presence.

❖ **Conduct effective interviews.** During your interviews with prospective agents, compile a complete profile of each candidate. Inquire about each agent's education, recent experience, personal integrity, availability, marketing strategy, and negotiation skills. Discuss your needs and the goals of your family – does this agent seem to offer the type of service that matches your needs? Trust your instincts, and don't be afraid to let an agent know that you have opted to pursue another option. Agents will understand that the fit has to be right on both ends of the equation.

❖ **Consider the specialists.** If your situation requires specific expertise, look for a specialist in that area (i.e. if you are planning to purchase a luxury home, a ranch property, or a short sale).

❖ **Stay local.** The importance of working with someone who knows your particular market inside and out cannot be overemphasized. Choose an agent who knows each street and each neighborhood in your new town, and who feels a personal connection to the area. Ideally, your agent will live in or near the immediate area.

❖ **Personality and availability are fundamental.** Even above sparkling credentials, an agent's personality traits and accessibility will make or break the experience for you. Make sure that both your personalities and your schedules coincide – you will likely be spending many hours a day with this person. There is no reason to work with even the most well qualified agent if his or her personality grates on your nerves, or if you have received a poor referral concerning that agent.

Common Pitfalls – Be mindful of these common, but preventable, mishaps as you navigate your relationship with your buyer's agent.

❖ **Dual representation** – Avoid working with an agent who is representing both the buyer and the seller in a single transaction. Though in some cases it may work, you ideally want to be fully represented by your agent; there is no reason to risk a conflict of interest. In certain circumstances it does occur, so if you find yourself in such a situation, just be sure that both buyer and seller have signed off, are in agreement, and understand what dual representation implies. After a long and difficult deal, as many can be, everyone wants to close the transaction and move on. Eliminate any issues ahead of time by being upfront, honest, and transparent.

❖ **Working with friends** – As with any business transaction, it can be unwise to work directly with close friends or family members. However, when it comes to buying or selling a new home, you want the best possible expert to represent you. If this person happens to be a relative or friend, who is also a local, full-time agent with experience, that is just fine; any agent who is at the top of her game and whom you trust will provide you with excellent service. However, whether you are a buyer or seller, you should avoid working with a friend or family member who works outside of your market. Out-of-market agents can pose an issue, as discussed earlier in this book. What is customary here may or may not be customary elsewhere. Heed the warning: transacting real estate is a specialized and highly emotional experience; partnering with the wrong agent can be a costly mistake.

❖ **Lofty promises** – Though this may seem self-evident, it is important to avoid agents who make grand claims without providing hard data to back them up. A serious and trustworthy agent will advise you based on recent experience within your market.

❖ **Expecting the agent to do all the work** – Don't forget that you have responsibilities of your own, just as your agent does. It is your duty to do your due diligence and communicate with your agent when you are uncertain about any facet of the process. For instance, ask him or her to define terms, explain a contract, divulge any hidden fees, or uncover certain facts about the market or the neighborhood. Although agents are legally bound to disclose everything they know about a particular property, it is up to you to be upfront about your desires, expectations, and concerns. Since your agent can't foresee your every want and need, do some homework on your own time – go visit properties and neighborhoods at all times of the day or night and figure out for yourself whether or not you could be happy living there. Chat with neighbors on the weekends, when most are home from work. Seek out any and all information that could affect your home-buying decision.

Buyer-Specific Questions Answered: Top Concerns for Home Buyers

1. How do I get my financial affairs in order? How can I ensure that I will obtain the best possible mortgage?

First things first: months before you begin to shop for dream homes or meet with a buyer's agent, well before you feel ready to begin looking for a home, it is essential that you take the time to review your finances. Consider your spending and saving habits, and make sure any payments are up to date.

Perhaps most importantly, secure copies of your **credit report** and take the necessary steps to improve it or amend any mistakes you may find. In order to secure a mortgage, you will need your credit history to be as spotless and solid as possible. The three major credit agencies, Experian, Equifax, and TransUnion, keep credit reports that delineate any issues you've had with credit or debt in the past. Websites such as MyFICO.com, Experian.com, FreeCreditReport.com and CreditKarma. com allow you to pay to access your credit reports and determine your **credit score**. In general, at any time of life, it is useful to order a report and check on your score every few years – small issues will arise on your report that you were unaware of. Indeed, errors in your credit reports are certainly possible and not uncommon; therefore, take action right away to contact the agencies and correct any potential mistakes you find. If the blemish is not removed—and it will take time to do so—your lender or mortgage broker will ask you to write a statement of explanation describing the reason for the late, missed, or erroneous mark on your credit report. Perhaps it was an oversight, a bill that was paid but not recorded as such, a gap from a time when you were out of work, and so on.

Once your credit score is in good shape, you can begin the process of selecting the ideal buyer's agent. It is important to choose your agent before taking the next financial step – getting preapproved for a loan by a lender. Preapproval puts you in a strong position to eventually make a serious offer to buy a home. Consult question number four below for more information on how to receive a preapproval and select a mortgage lender.

2.   How do I select the right location in which to buy?

Though you are surely itching to discover that ideal home, there are many other factors involved in making your choice, apart from the home itself. Experienced real estate agents know that, before a buyer falls in love with a specific home, he must choose the city or neighborhood first. Yes, the house itself—including its layout, its size and the number of bedrooms and bathrooms—represents a significant variable. But, as they say, location is everything. If you have decided to move to the Bay Area, you must first decide if you want to live in the East Bay, the South Bay, the North Bay, or in Contra Costa County.

Once you have chosen the broader area, you will want to hone in on specific towns or cities. For instance, in Oakland, do you prefer Crocker Highlands, Oakmore, Rockridge, or Montclair (to name just a few)? Of course your budget will also play a part in your decision. In the North Bay, i.e. in Marin County, do you prefer to be close to San Francisco, thereby purchasing a home in such towns as Sausalito, Mill Valley, Tiburon, or Belvedere, or do you prefer the warmer weather in Greenbrae, San Anselmo, San Rafael, or Novato? Further north still, you may find the Sonoma or Napa Valley a perfect place to reside. Or, if you are interested in living in a university town, Berkeley might be your first choice. If public schools and a small town community are of particular interest, Piedmont, a small town located in the foothills of the East Bay, might be your best choice. Should you prefer more land, warmer weather, and a more suburban environment, you may enjoy Orinda, Lafayette, or any of the other many communities out past the Caldecott Tunnel off of Highways 24 and 680. If you work in the Silicon Valley, then you will want to focus your search on one of the many towns or cities in the South Bay.

When selecting your ideal community, especially consider its social and economic features. For instance, what are the recreational and cultural benefits of living in this town? If you have children, you will want to know what activities and diversions are available for kids in the community. Is the neighborhood close to local schools? What is the quality of schools in this district? Think about your commute to and from work – if your commute will be relatively long, will the perks of living in this area be worth the daily trip back and forth? Then, ask yourself if the area is conducive to the lifestyle you lead. Does it lend itself to raising a family, to single life, to retirement living, or to your particular style of living?

Regardless of whether or not you currently have school-age children, living within good school districts is a major asset. Distinguished schools are a primary selling point when it comes time for you to sell this new home, and thus help your home to gain value. To investigate the quality of schools in your area, we recommend researching online rankings (such as those compiled each year by the U.S. News & World Report) or requesting reports of local test scores, graduation rates, and college acceptances from the schools themselves.

Note: When you finally get down to selecting a specific home you are interested in, it is very important to confirm with the school district itself. Do not rely on online websites as confirmation. We once had a listing in Piedmont that was falsely displayed on the Internet as though it fed to Oakland's Skyline High School and not to Piedmont High School. Had this been the case, the value of the home would have been dramatically different. Again, be sure to speak to a live person and document your finding. You wouldn't want to purchase a home in an area that you were led to believe belongs to a specific school district when in fact it doesn't, if this is of importance to you.

Next, it is very important to look for economic vitality in any community. Ideally your town will rely on a diverse array of employers, will contain young people, families and elderly couples, and will evidence low unemployment rates and stable incomes.

Whether a neighborhood is quiet enough, safe enough, small enough, or friendly enough (among other concerns) is ultimately up to you. While an agent can advise you on all aspects of a given neighborhood in your market, it is your job to determine the area's livability for yourself and your family. For this reason, it is important to visit a property or neighborhood you like during both daytime and nighttime hours, on week days and on weekends, and to speak with as diverse a selection of its inhabitants as you can find. The ultimate decision is up to you!

3. How do I interview a buyer's agent?

Before conducting your interviews with potential buyer's agents, do some basic preparation. Know what sort of agent you are hoping to find, what sort of house, neighborhood, and community you are hoping to live in, and make a note of your estimated price range. Throughout the interview, expect that the agent will ask questions of you as well. Pay attention to what questions he or she asks – is the agent discerning? Is he or she a good listener? Does he or she seem knowledgeable about the market, and eager to assist you? Think of the meeting as an opportunity for both you and the agent to assess the personality and goals of the other, in order to find out if you can see yourselves working together productively throughout the admittedly stressful process.

In the pages that follow, you will find a convenient and exhaustive sample questionnaire, which suggests over twenty questions that will guide you in your interviews. We suggest that you photocopy this questionnaire and bring it with you each time you meet a new agent. It will help you to determine essential information about each agent, including their Experience, Marketing, Feedback, Personality and Character, Industry Connections, and Results, among other topics. If you cover the topics proposed in our questionnaire, you will be able to furnish a complete and accurate picture of each agent you interview. In addition to asking these suggested questions, we recommend that you discuss loan preapproval with each agent. If you have yet to receive approval for a loan—which is in fact advisable, since your agent can help you to secure the best lender—ask the agent which banks or lenders she typically works with and why. She should be able to refer you to one or more banks, loan agents, or mortgage brokers in your area, taking into consideration your personal financial picture in order to match you with at least two mortgage consultants or brokers who would be ideal for you.

Just as our questionnaire indicates, it is crucial that you request a list of references (namely, recent clients from the past several months) from each potential agent. Contact several past clients in order to gain an insider perspective on the quality of service provided by each agent.

DiMaggio's Questionnaire for Interviewing a Buyer's Agent (a.k.a. Selling Agent)

Experience

1. What is your education and training?

    _____

    _____

    _____

    _____

2. For how many years have you been actively working in the industry? Are you a full-time or a part-time agent?

    _____

    _____

    _____

    _____

3. If you are a new agent, do you work under the supervision of a broker? Is your broker readily accessible to you?

    _____

    _____

    _____

    _____

4. What is your preferred negotiation strategy?

    _____

    _____

    _____

    _____

5. What qualities or experiences set you apart from your competition?

    _____

    _____

_____

_____

Feedback

6. When, how and how often should I expect to communicate with you? How frequently will you update me on new listings?

_____

_____

_____

_____

7. May I contact a list of recent references (preferably all clients from within the past six to 12 months) to discuss your qualifications?

_____

_____

_____

_____

Industry Connections

8. How familiar are you with this area, its inhabitants and organizations? Do you live in this neighborhood, or have you sold many homes here recently?

_____

_____

_____

_____

9. Are you familiar with other reliable service professionals who work in this area?

_____

_____

_____

_____

Partnership

10. How big is your staff? Will I be working predominantly with you or with your assistants?

_____

_____

_____

_____

11. What are your hours, and how flexible is your schedule?

_____

_____

_____

_____

12. How do you prefer to communicate (i.e. via text, phone call, email)?

_____

_____

_____

_____

Personality and Character

13. How do you demonstrate integrity to your clients?

_____

_____

_____

_____

14. How do you ensure that you give your buyers honest advice?

_____

_____

_____

_____

Results

15. How much do you charge, and what kind of guarantee do you offer?

_____

_____

_____

_____

16. What is your plan of action for my specific needs?

_____

_____

_____

_____

17. What else do I need to know that I have yet to ask?

_____

_____

_____

_____

4.   How do I choose a mortgage lender?

Selecting your **mortgage lender** is a very important decision, since mortgages often take between fifteen and forty years to pay off. Now that you have selected your stellar buyer's agent, rely on his or her expertise to assist you in this choice. Your agent should provide you with two or three referrals, although he or she may already have identified a specific lender based on your personal financial situation.

It is essential to work with a local lender from your market who is familiar to your agent. The lender must be someone your agent trusts to get the deal done. A reliable, well-known local agent may be able to grant you certain benefits (such as short-term contingencies) and will give you a greater likelihood of having your offer accepted; on the other hand, working with an unheard-of agent from the Internet will make things slower and riskier for you. While websites such as E-loan.com and Bankrate.com may seem like tempting options, top agents know that it is important not to get your approval from just any source. The lender you go with will make a difference to the agent hearing your offer. If the listing agent is unsure of the lender's performance or knowledge of what is customary in our micro-market, it may mean the difference between winning and losing the home.

In our local seller's market especially, it matters who you work with – all banks and lenders are *not* created equal. If your lender is a trusted and reliable source, you have a greater chance of having your offer to buy a home accepted. Furthermore, with an online lending source you will have no control over the timetable; when you need critical information or documentation from your lender, you won't have twenty-four hours to wait – you will need immediate feedback. It's clear then that you will need to work with a real live person for quick responses and local insights. If you do wish to use your own preferred lender, bank, or mortgage broker, your agent should interview him or her. Here are a few important qualities we look for: 1) Is the lender on-call and accessible at all times? 2) Does he or she return calls, emails, and text messages promptly? And

3) Does the lender have access to local appraisers and understand the importance of using appraisers from the same area code as the home you are offering on? It should go without saying that the lender must provide his or her mobile number and be accessible on weekends. Real estate doesn't stand still outside the hours of 9 AM and 5 PM, or during weekends, dinnertime, or Sunday brunch.

In the same way that it is risky to partner with online lending sites, it is never a good idea to work with an out-of-area lender. Here are just a few reasons why: out-of-area lenders don't know your specific market, don't have relationships with local appraisers or the confidence of local agents, and simply do not have the necessary experience in your market to assist nervous clients or review appraisals. Using an out-of-area lender can do just as much harm as using an out-of-area Realtor®. If you want to position yourself as a winner, then follow our lead. You'll be happy you did.

That being said, discuss with your agent the various advantages and benefits of the different options available to you. You might choose to work with a **mortgage broker**, a sort of middleman who is the conduit between the buyer and a lender. A mortgage broker keeps track of the interest rates of several lenders at once. Mortgage brokers can therefore go to multiple banks and lending institutions and shop around to get you the best loan, which often makes this option a popular one. Or, you may decide to employ a **loan agent**, or loan consultant, who works solely with one particular bank with the main objective of recommending individual and business loan applications for approval. Whatever you decide, be sure to depend upon the referrals given by your agent, who will help you locate the best lender to suit your needs.

5.   What can I realistically afford?
      Before getting your heart set on a specific property or type of home, it is beneficial to determine what you can in fact afford. To help you estimate the amount you would be able to offer for a home, consider utilizing one of the many online calculators that determine the sum for you. These

calculators take into account your income, debts, and other expenses before suggesting a dollar amount.

In addition, receiving preapproval from a lender will inform you as to what type of loan is within your reach, which will then indicate what you can afford. Buyers absolutely must be preapproved for a loan before making an offer on any home in our competitive area. Also consider the size of your down payment – you should be prepared to come up with roughly 20% of the home's price on your own as your down payment. If you are able to offer even more, you will likely qualify for a larger loan.

One common axiom suggests buying a property that costs about two-and-a-half to three times your annual salary. While this calculation may be a useful indicator, you should by no means rely upon sweeping generalizations such as this; instead, work together with your agent and lender to determine a viable price range.

When you are assessing what homes you can afford, don't fool yourself into thinking that the home's price tag is all that you'll need to budget for. Other fees and closing costs include the appraisal fee, loan fees, inspection fees and more – don't forget to factor these in to your estimates. Once you have decided on a budget, it's time for you to begin the exciting process of house hunting!

6. What is a home inspection and is it necessary?

Once you have made an offer to purchase the home of your choosing and have had your offer accepted by the sellers, you will enter into the **escrow period**. A home that is "in escrow" refers to a home sale that is pending. In our area, a typical escrow period is between 21 and 30 days. During this escrow period, you will typically opt to conduct a **home inspection** to make sure you can afford to make the necessary repairs, maintenance, and/or home improvements. More importantly, the inspector will help you to understand the components and systems in the home you are about to buy. The home inspector and agent will also help you to prioritize what is most important to do now and what types of repairs or upgrades can be postponed for a later date. In the back of the home inspection report will be a list of items to address, beginning with the most pressing and most important. The inspection will help you to identify any issues with the property that may arise down the road, and will give you peace of mind about the status of your new investment. Even though the bank will conduct its own **home appraisal** in order to finalize your loan, it is usually recommended that you hire your own home inspector. Oftentimes, in a fast-paced market, a seller will furnish a home inspection report for interested buyers in advance. If you are not satisfied with the report provided by the seller, you may opt to pre-inspect a home using your own home inspector, prior to the offer date. This tactic puts the buyer in a more desirable position in a multiple-offer situation. However, always obtain permission from the seller's agent before you pre-inspect. Some agents will allow it and others may not.

During your pending or escrow period, you will address all **contingencies** that pertain to the sale of the home, including Appraisal, Loan, and the Physical or Home Inspection Contingency (read more about contingencies in Chapter 10). If you as a buyer have this contingency, you can inspect anything you would like. This often includes inspections of individual systems: the foundation, the roofing, and the electrical, as well as verifications of police reports, Megan's Law information, and any additional data that the buyer deems important. It is highly advised, indeed

necessary, that you yourself are present at the inspection. You want to be the expert on your own new home so that you know where everything is located and what future improvements you can expect to budget for. If, after the inspection report has been completed, anything is not to your liking, you can then instruct your agent to attempt to negotiate for a monetary credit—an unusual occurrence in our fast-paced current market— or to request a cancellation of contract. Though an outright cancellation

rarely happens, certain circumstances may make it necessary; if it is, a buyer can receive 100% of their deposit back. (Note: Each circumstance is different and may not be crystal clear or as cut-and-dry as you may think, regarding the return of your security deposit. You will have to rely on your agent and, if necessary, an attorney for clarity and guidance.)

Sometimes, in a competitive situation, buyers may opt not to conduct a home inspection because they are already satisfied with the various reports and inspections provided by the seller in the disclosure packet, and wish to be as competitive as possible. Should this be the case, the buyers then choose to be **non-contingent**, thereby waiving their right to the Home Inspection Contingency.

If, on the other hand, the buyer is not comfortable with being non-contingent, is a first-time home buyer or is otherwise unsure of how to proceed, we recommend that your agent includes a 3-5 day Home Inspection Contingency. Of course, this is dependent upon how connected your agent is with his or her local service providers and home inspectors. While other agents may suggest a 7-10 day or even 17-day Home Inspection Contingency, a shorter contingency period always presents a more competitive offer. Buyers may be concerned that a period of 3-5 days is too short a time to conduct a thorough inspection of the home; but, if your agent is part of a connected network of professional contacts and resources, then he or she will be able to get the job done. Successful agents are the ones who cultivate solid connections and strong relationships with their home inspectors and other vendors.

In our competitive local housing market, home inspections have become important tools. Since buyers' offers are more competitive when they are non-contingent on the Home Inspection Contingency, some buyers will invest money in a house even before they know they have secured the home – some buyers choose to conduct a pre-inspection on a property they love, even before they have made an offer or had it accepted. Today's local buyers are willing to put money up on a property before they have secured that property because they know that this could pay off for them in the end. After conducting a pre-inspection, buyers can put forth an offer with no contingencies attached, which signifies an easy, quick close to the sellers and provides them with the peace of mind to move on with their plans. This is how many buyers are getting homes, and, depending on your situation, pre-inspecting a home can be a good investment.

House Hunting

How do I locate properties for sale?

Aside from driving through prospective neighborhoods or performing your own online research, the best way to locate properties for sale is through your buyer's agent. As soon as you have hired an agent to represent you, he or she will set you up to receive via email daily updates on new properties that hit the market. You will then receive alerts whenever a realty office enters a new listing into the MLS, the local Multiple Listing Service. This alert system is known as **First Alert** or Property Alert. The First Alert system will also notify you whenever changes, updates, corrections, or new photographs of a property are uploaded to the MLS. Properties are sometimes entered into the MLS while the Realtor® is still working to get professional photographs taken and uploaded. Oftentimes buyers will contact their agents requesting more photos of a given property, but with First Alert, buyers will be informed as soon as this process occurs. A buyer using this system can also typically categorize properties they like or want to discard.

Your agent will also send you a list of the local open houses occurring that weekend. In the East Bay, all open houses tend to take place on Sundays between 2:00 PM and 4:30 or 5:00 PM. Buyers typically choose to visit properties on their own during the Sunday open house; if they view a property or properties that they especially like, the agent will then schedule another time to view said property(ies) with the buyers so they can discuss its features and review its disclosures in private. Sunday open houses are a wonderful way for buyers to see who else is looking to move into the community and to get a strong feeling about various neighborhoods on their own. A buyer shouldn't be intimidated by the activity and foot traffic at a Sunday open house–especially a property's first—since many of the people who stop by are neighbors, people who tour open houses as a hobby, or potential sellers seeking an agent, rather than other buyers competing for the home.

What do I do when I discover a property I like?

Because our market moves so quickly, it is ideal to let your agent know right away that you are interested in a property so he or she can keep an eye on it. When a buyer expresses interest in a home, the buyer's agent will contact the seller's agent in order to obtain a **disclosure packet**. The disclosure packet is a list of documents and inspection reports pertaining to a home, including a property history documented by the seller in the form of questionnaires. The buyer should then review the disclosure packet carefully, and ask any relevant questions of his agent. The agent will contact the seller's agent regarding any updates in disclosure items or any potential **preemptive offers** (see page 177). The agent will keep the buyer informed as to an offer date, if any, along with any updates, changes, or new information. While some seller's agents will hear your offer as soon as you have written it (known as "as written"), most seller's agents will have a specified **offer date**, on which day they will hear offers from all interested parties at a designated time, one offer at a time. An offer is typically accepted on this same, pre-determined day. Offer dates—determined by the seller and his or her agent—are often set in this area for the Tuesday or Wednesday preceding the second Sunday open house. An agent usually sets an offer date only after they have received multiple requests for a disclosure packet; if a home is not as popular then the agent won't set a specific offer date. Offer dates cannot be set if there is no interest. Buyers' interest is what dictates the market. On the offer date for the property that you like (should there be one), your agent will personally present your written offer to the seller(s) and/or seller's agent. Before doing so, you (with your agent's help) will need to go through the home's disclosure packet multiple times, ask any questions, gain clarity and understanding, and decide if you will write any contingencies into your offer. In a typical situation, you will hear a response to your offer—i.e. whether it is accepted or rejected—on the same day that you present your offer.

CHAPTER 5:
ALL ABOUT SELLING

Given today's hot seller's market and improved local job market, perhaps you and your family have decided it's time to sell your home. If so, congratulations! This is a wonderful time to be a seller.

When considering your own individual motivations for selling—whether it's a job move, you're sizing up, sizing down, or moving to a new community—keep in mind that selling a home is an overwhelming undertaking. Home sellers are often surprised at how emotional the process can be. But rest assured: despite the challenges, selling a home is not rocket science. Remember that it only takes one buyer to sell. You only need to connect with that one specific buyer for whom your home is the perfect fit. Furthermore, now more than ever, it's not a question of if your home will sell, but when – and if you have the right, qualified agent working with you, the whole process will be completed in no time. Don't let skewed Internet-based facts and figures—based on the proceedings in other markets—deceive you; you need a living, breathing, professional agent on your team. Choosing your real estate agent is arguably the most important step of all. So how do you identify that experienced, stellar, matchless listing agent?

Choosing the Seller's Agent

The listing agent, also known as the **seller's agent**, will be your one-stop shop for all direction and advice, the right-hand man (or woman) who will guide you through the process of selling your home. Your agent can both simplify your life and deftly manage any obstacles that may arise, or he or she can turn your home-selling experience into an unpleasant ordeal. To be able to distinguish a world-class agent from a second-rate amateur, consider the following advice.

Before You Begin Looking – Keep these tips in mind before you even begin your search for the perfect agent:

- ❖ **You do in fact need an agent.** While it is theoretically possible to sell your home without one, it is rarely, if ever, a rewarding venture for the seller. True, without hiring an agent you may potentially save some money, but you would also need to advertise and market your home yourself, and be available to show it at any time of the day or night. Ask yourself: am I knowledgeable enough about the customs and paperwork involved to sell my home without the help of a professional? In almost every case, hiring a listing agent will spare you a large headache, and will place you and your home in a much better position to make a successful sale. It will be no surprise to hear that we live in a litigious society; making the wrong move or forgetting or declining to disclose defects about your home could very well end up costing you more than an agent's commission in the end – not to mention the money you may have left on the table and the enormous amount of time being taken away from your daily life.

- ❖ **Be prepared to interview prospective agents.** Before selecting an agent, you should ideally interview two or three qualified candidates. Avoid interviewing multiple agents from the same company when possible, in order to minimize potential rivalries. Don't be afraid to ask the difficult questions!

- ❖ **It is not your agent's job to tell you how much your house will sell for.** The market will dictate that one! Remind yourself from the start that, as far as pricing goes, your agent's responsibility is to provide you with a comparative market analysis (CMA) and to suggest a price range based on comparable sales over the last three months. In some areas where inventory is scarce, agents will have to go back further, and this is most often the case. You should be honest with yourself and work with your agent to determine the most suitable asking, or "listing," price for your home. As noted above, the market dictates price, not your agent: the interest of prospective buyers will indicate whether or not your chosen price is fair. Information is readily available to both buyers and sellers; there is no hiding from the true value of your home. The price the seller wants or thinks is reasonable is not relevant, and that's just the way it is.

- ❖ **Don't allow yourself to be deceived.** If you have already decided to automatically go with the agent who promises you the highest selling price for your home, you are setting yourself up for disappointment. The agent that suggests the highest price may be exaggerating; be prepared to ask for data to back up these claims. We refer to this as "buying a listing." Some agents will attempt to buy a listing by giving you an inflated opinion of value. This only hurts, not helps.

- ❖ **Only about 10% of the agents do 90% of the business.** This industry adage largely rings true: the top 10% of real estate agents get the vast majority of the business because they have a reputation for being hard-working, experienced, and ethical professionals whom people can trust.

The Selection Process – While you're out on the hunt for the ideal seller's agent, bear in mind the following:

- ❖ **Look to your neighbors.** It is often wise to begin by surveying your neighborhood to find out where the For Sale signs are coming from. Is one company or one individual agent favored above others? Does this company or agent seem to provide effective marketing tools? How do they present their homes? Also, never discount word of mouth references from trusted friends and neighbors! Referrals are a wonderful source for both buyers and sellers, and certainly work to the agent's best advantage as well. When someone you respect gives you a reference—whether positive or negative—trust that reference. This is not a decision you want to regret later on, so take advantage of the learning experiences of others. As a case in point, one seller whom we interviewed mentioned that they had received a poor review about another agent; they ended up choosing this agent anyway and, in the end, had a less than desirable experience.

❖ **Narrow your search.** Seek out agents who specialize in the type of service you need (i.e. single family homes, condos, luxury homes, etc.).

❖ **In interviews, know what you're looking for.** The most important characteristics any agent brings to the table are: his or her experience, education, trustworthiness, networking potential (i.e. affiliation with reliable and readily available contractors), accessibility, marketing plan, and negotiation and communication skills. Personality is especially important in this industry; all sellers want an agent who's an assertive and diligent worker, but without being an overly aggressive type. It is equally important that any agent is well respected amongst her colleagues; fellow agents will be happy to work with an agent who is a team player rather than someone who is always on the defense. During your interviews, respect your gut feelings – selling a home is stressful, and you want an agent who will make the process easier and calmer for you. Take note: the agent whom you are interviewing does want to help you but does not read minds. If you have certain needs or opinions, or agree or disagree with something she has said, be honest. It's truly the best and only way you can understand the process. The agent may maintain a firm position, but at least you will understand the reasons why and not be irritated or frustrated by what the agent is saying.

❖ **Marketing sells homes.** Focus on the agent's proven marketing skills. Any successful marketing plan should contain at least the following: professional signage, staging advice, weekly newspaper advertisements, MLS exposure, four-color flyers, 2+ open houses, and direct mail to immediate neighbors. Rather than tracking down the agent with the cheapest commission, it is often beneficial to select an agent with a large advertising budget who works for a company with large-scale exposure. This will give your home greater exposure to the largest number of buyers. However, even if the agent's company advertises, you will still want to be sure to work with a proactive agent who markets and advertises as well.

❖ **Stay local.** An agent who either lives in or frequently sells homes in your neighborhood will have insider knowledge of the particular challenges that may arise in your area. An ideal seller's agent is personally passionate about your neighborhood, and knows it backwards and forwards, inside and out.

❖ **Learn from the past.** Look at your agent's history and past track record – does he or she consistently sell homes below the asking price? If so, why? Asking why is important. If a home sells for lower than the asking price is may be that the agent over-priced the home, the seller didn't take the advice or recommendations of the agent, or the home contained features that are unappealing to certain buyers (i.e. too many stairs, lack of a level garden, a property that is too vertical, etc.).

❖ **Sign a contract.** You will need to sign a formal **listing agreement** with your chosen agent. In today's hot market, a 90-day contract is common. Depending on the amount of work to be done prior to market, you may need to extend your contract from 90 to 120 days, allowing enough time for inspections and renovations. This contract will address the compensation requested by your agent, among other details.

Common Pitfalls – Avoid these all-too-common snags in order to ensure the best possible partnership with your listing agent.

❖ **Cheap commission fees** – While it's tempting to automatically select the agent with the lowest fee, it's also healthy to be skeptical of cheap rates. Consider why an agent's fee may be lower than that of the competition: does she have less experience? Is she desperate for work? Does she provide poor service? Is she unconnected or inexperienced? Furthermore, keep in mind that you almost always get what you pay for. An agent with a cheaper fee has a smaller budget, will most definitely cut corners, and will therefore not be prepared to properly market your house. With a major financial decision like this, you don't want to take any risks. A bigger commission can in fact help you, since it gives the agent greater incentive (and means) to advocate tirelessly on your behalf, in addition to the agent(s) bringing in an offer.

❖ **Working with friends** – In many areas of life, it's often best to keep business life and personal relationships separate. When it comes to real estate representation, leave it to your best judgment. This means that, while it may be generally inadvisable to do business with a close friend or family member, what is most important is to choose the best agent for your needs. Should you wish to consider a friend for the job, evaluate him or her as you would any other candidate – and don't be afraid to say "no." If he or she turns out to be the leading candidate, then go for it!

❖ **Hearing everything you want to hear** – Be wary of the agent who seems to be merely telling you what you want to hear, rather than disclosing the honest truth. If your agent suggests a wonderfully high price for your home and it ends up sitting on the market, keep in mind that you're only helping other similar houses to look more appealing in comparison. Look for the agent who promises to price your home fairly; when the price is right, buyers will come flocking. You really cannot underprice a home.

❖ **Dual representation** – Although there is an exception to every rule, it is probably best, in order to avoid any conflicts of interest, that your agent represents you alone and not the homebuyer as well. Your agent should have a clear personal stake in your individual success as a seller.

* ❖ **Communication misunderstandings** – Keep avenues of communication wide open with your agent. Make plain from the very beginning how often you wish to receive updates from him or her, such that there can be no confusion or expensive misunderstandings later on. Your agent cannot read minds, and any good agent should want to make sure you have the best and most seamless experience.

Seller-Specific Questions Answered: Top Concerns for Home Sellers

1. How do I interview a seller's agent?

To make the most of your interviews with potential agents, it is recommended that you come prepared. Bring a list of the essential questions you want answers to, and be ready to answer questions about your own motivations for selling, about your home, and about what you seek in a partnership with your agent. You and the agent should be interviewing each other, in a sense, to determine whether or not you would form a productive partnership. "Partnership" is the key word – you should consider yourselves a team.

An exhaustive sample questionnaire, complete with over twenty questions, is provided below. This questionnaire contains the questions we feel are most important in determining whether a listing agent is right for you. The questions range in topic from Experience, Marketing, Feedback, Personality and Character, and Industry Connections, to Partnership, Money Matters, and Results. Please feel free to photocopy this questionnaire and bring it with you to any agent interviews you conduct.

As our questionnaire indicates, it is vital that you request a reference list from each prospective seller's agent you interview. After contacting and speaking with all of his or her recent clients, you will have a much better understanding of the quality of service provided by the agent. If an agent is confident in his or her own value as a professional, he or she will not shy away from the opportunity to provide you with reliable references.

DiMaggio's Questionnaire for Interviewing a Seller's Agent (a.k.a. Listing Agent)

Experience

1. How long have you been in the real estate business?
    Are you a full-time agent?

    _____

    _____

    _____

    _____

2. How connected are you in the industry? With your local
    real estate community? With Realtors® outside of the area?

    _____

    _____

    _____

    _____

3. What are the most important career-related things you
    have done or learned in the past year?

    _____

    _____

    _____

    _____

4. What sets you apart from the competition?

    _____

    _____

    _____

    _____

Marketing

5. How, when, and where will you advertise my listing?

    _____

    _____

    _____

    _____

6. What does your marketing package consist of? Do you
    employ direct mail campaigns; will you place a sign in my
    yard, etc.? Do you believe a For Sale sign is important?
    Is it more for you or for me?

    _____

    _____

    _____

    _____

7. How do you make use of the Internet? To what extent do
    you employ social media?

    _____

    _____

    _____

    _____

8. How often do you typically hold open houses?

    _____

    _____

    _____

    _____

Feedback

9. What sort of feedback will you be providing me with, and how often?

_____

_____

_____

_____

10. Will you allow me to review documents (such as the listing agreement and agency disclosure) ahead of time?

_____

_____

_____

_____

11. May I have a list of references, i.e. all recent clients from the past 6-12 months, whom I can contact to discuss your qualifications? Will you also provide me with a list of the 5+ most recent sales you have made?

_____

_____

_____

_____

Industry Connections

12. Will you recommend to me other industry professionals (such as mortgage brokers and home inspectors)? Why are you confident in recommending these individuals?

_____

_____

_____

_____

13. Are you familiar with this area/town/neighborhood? Do you live nearby, or do you frequently sell homes here?

_____

_____

_____

_____

Partnership

14. Do you work with a staff? Will I primarily be dealing with you, or with others who work for or with you?

_____

_____

_____

_____

15. Will you be available to attend to my needs on a reasonably prompt basis?

_____

_____

_____

_____

Personality and Character

16. Do you consider customer service and friendliness to be essential aspects of your profession? Do you seek to be transparent and communicative with your clients?

_____

_____

_____

_____

17. Why can I trust in your integrity and character?

_____
_____
_____
_____

Money Matters

18. How much do you charge? Do you offer any discounted fees, or will you match other agents' fees, should they be lower?

_____
_____
_____
_____

Results

19. What is your average list-price-to-sales-price ratio?

_____
_____
_____
_____

20. What reason or reasons would cause a home not to sell?

_____
_____
_____
_____

21. What else do I need to know that I have yet to ask you?

_____
_____
_____
_____

2.   What is the pre-listing home inspection and why is it necessary?

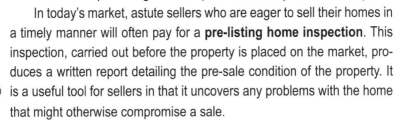

In today's market, astute sellers who are eager to sell their homes in a timely manner will often pay for a **pre-listing home inspection**. This inspection, carried out before the property is placed on the market, produces a written report detailing the pre-sale condition of the property. It is a useful tool for sellers in that it uncovers any problems with the home that might otherwise compromise a sale.

Pre-listing home inspections typically expedite a sale. By identifying and addressing obstacles early on, a seller will know, prior to closing: what issues exist, what can and should be fixed before listing, and what will need to be disclosed to the buyer.

Early inspections benefit all parties involved. They speed up the selling process for sellers and can be used to justify a higher asking price. For buyers, the pre-listing inspection provides peace of mind and confidence, demonstrating the integrity and soundness of a property that interests them.

With or without a pre-listing inspection, buyers may still bring in their own inspectors. Still, as a seller you don't want some significant complication to turn up during the buyer's last-minute inspection; this could persuade them to back out of a sale. Rather, you will benefit from knowing from the get-go what it is that you're working with, so that you can make the home most appealing to your buyers. Moreover, once you are in contract on your own new home and are potentially paying two mortgages, having a buyer back out due to issues that could have been revealed and addressed earlier can be costly. Our goal as your agents is to minimize, as best we can, any potential issues. This guidance and counseling comes from years of experience.

Keep in mind that the inspector you hire will always find something wrong with the property – know at the outset that this is natural. Only major deficiencies—or a stubborn unwillingness to negotiate on your part—will threaten a deal. Buyers will likely be willing to overlook the little things once they fall in love with your home.

 During your inspection, it helps to be upfront in advance about any problems you are aware of in your home. They will be discovered sooner or later regardless. "Location, location, location" is to a buyer as "disclose, disclose, disclose" is to a seller. Inspectors will primarily check the home for: signs of water damage, including leaks and mold; termites or structural problems; problems with heating and cooling; the condition of the roof and sewer; rodent infestations; the presence of smoke and CO detectors; and plumbing and electrical issues. They will also examine any do-it-yourself projects or renovations you've completed to ensure their workmanship and durability. The inspector will then provide you with any suggestions for further inspections they deem necessary; you can then hire a specialized service provider who will inspect specific systems and provide a bid with the cost to repair any outdated or damaged systems. After considering these costs, it is up to you to either take on the repairs prior to market or to pass them on to the buyer in the form of documented disclosures. If you choose the latter option, the inspector's report will notify the buyer as to what costs they can expect to face. In general, the more items you fix prior to market, the better it will be for you. People will recognize that your home is in great shape and will take interest. If the suggested repair is minor, fix it now!

 To facilitate any and all inspections of your home, consider the following suggestions: inform the inspector ahead of time about known problem areas and of anything else about your home you think he should know. Clean out spaces in front of appliances, sink pipes, and electrical panels and empty out your washer, dryer, dishwasher, and stove to allow the inspector to access them with ease. Clear a pathway to your attic and basement, and to the underside of your house. Unlock any gates and side doors, and provide any documentation of repairs you've conducted. Moreover, when your buyers are conducting their own inspection, vacate the home with your children and your pets in tow; this allows the buyers to speak candidly with the inspector without the distraction of the homeowners present. (Note: At all times, sellers should always excuse themselves from their home while it is being shown or inspected. Buyers will spend less time in the home when a seller is present. The goal is to allow buyers to connect with your home—which will hopefully become their new home.)

3.   How do I choose an optimal asking price for my home?

It is extremely important to price your home properly from the get-go. In fact, the key to receiving the highest possible amount for your home is pricing, or the original asking price.

When deciding on a suitable asking price for your property, the single most important factor to consider is the assortment of comparable homes in your neighborhood – those currently for sale, those recently sold, and those that were recently for sale. It is important to stay within the realistic range established by these homes. While considering your comps, pay special attention to the sold comparable homes. Your sales price will eventually be subject to an appraisal based on the sale prices of these sold homes. Appraisers have guidelines and attempt to examine homes that have sold in the past three months for comparison.

Though this may not be the case everywhere, overpricing is detrimental to marketing strategy in today's East Bay real estate market. When a home is priced too high, the seller often wonders why no offers have been presented. This is because potential buyers are concerned about offending the seller, and therefore won't propose a lower offer. Rather than suggest a price that is lower than what the seller is asking, buyers will wait around until the seller finally decides to reduce the asking price. This same cycle occurs time and again in local markets when homes are listed too high, and only hurts the seller in the end.

To avoid this sort of setback, listen to your agent and heed his or her advice. The price range she suggests is based on her experience with this market and her conversations with other agents about how the market is currently behaving. She will suggest a certain range because she knows that it is a fair and accurate one, and one that will bring in offers and get the home sold.

Sellers often ask their agents, "What will my home sell for?" While your agent would love to be able to see into the future and give you an exact answer, any agent can only speculate from closed or recent sales – i.e. homes currently "in escrow," or "pending." A home that is pending is a recent and valuable comp. (If you are a buyer, your agent should ask the listing agents of those pending or sold homes how many offers they received and if they will share the sale price, or approximate sale price, of that home. This tells us how many active buyers are looking at the exact time, in the same price range as you.) Since offers in our local market are typically heard all on one specified day, your agent cannot tell you what your home will sell for. He or she can speculate as to a price range or what percentage over the asking price the sale price might be, but this is simply a best guess. No one knows what a home will sell for until offers are heard. Since the seller's agent and the seller(s) will not be hearing offers until a specific offer date, they will not know any more than a buyer knows. (Note: The only way to estimate the number of buyers who may be writing offers is to make a best guess based on the number of buyers who have requested disclosure packets. Agents will usually share how many packets have been requested. However, oftentimes buyers and their agents don't even confirm with the seller's agent until the last minute, so it's a guessing game right until the end – a surprise to all.)

Instead of waiting in vain for your agent to come up with some magic number, take matters into your own hands. It can be useful to visit other open houses in your area in order to investigate the competition and educate yourself on pricing. For the sake of propriety, you may choose to inform the agent present at each open house that you've stopped by because you yourself are contemplating selling – not as a potential buyer. After this, keep the dialogue going – opening up a conversation with an agent is always advantageous, so don't shy away. You never know what you might learn. When you do visit other homes for sale, keep in mind that it is dangerous to mentally compare two homes that aren't truly comparable. You may

see a home on the market that looks like yours and is listed higher. Before assuming that your agent didn't advise you correctly and that you should be asking more for your house too, consider the many factors that determine a home's value. For example, if your home has a larger yard, but their home has one extra bedroom and a more spacious garage, your home may not be as similar as

Locally, buyers tend to favor the following assets: easy access from the kitchen to the garden, a level outdoor space for entertaining, three or more upstairs bedrooms, and fewer stairs in general.

you think. Certain assets in a home are more desirable than other assets, and it is not up to your agent to regulate these market trends. A few of the features that may make a home less desirable to East Bay Area buyers are: too many stairs to the front door, a multi-level floor plan, lack of a level garden, poor access to the garden from the home or kitchen, a tight floor plan, no master bathroom, a dated home, and significant foundation or pest issues. While these factors may detract from your home's value, many features enhance the value of a property.

When marketing a home, an agent should always do her best to highlight the home's best features, but should be honest with the seller in private while you are considering the asking price. Don't take offense, as you want an agent who will provide her honest opinion. By all means, dialogue with your agent and share your opinions, but be sure to listen and hear what the agent is sharing with you as well.

When pricing your home, you should also be careful not to rely too heavily on the price per square foot. This guide should be used as a general indicator and not as a decisive factor. Other factors that determine the price of a home include: the location, the condition of the home, the layout, the state of the yard, and the number of stairs.

Some dishonest agents attempt to "buy your listing" – in other words, to encourage you to set an unrealistically high asking price just for the sake of securing your business. Don't allow yourself to be tempted by such schemes. If you have selected an agent you can trust and enjoying working with, this should not be a concern. In most cases, you and your agent will work together for a month or more before you even begin to discuss the final listing price of your home.

Above all, you want to avoid having to reduce your price. Since you have one chance to make a good impression, reducing a home's price shows that the home was overvalued in the first place. Buyers will see that your price was reduced and will question the motivation behind this. It will create a blemish of sorts on your home's reputation. Under-pricing a home is valuable in a seller's market, but this strategy cannot be utilized in all markets. A seller and his or her agent must take into account the current market conditions to determine the best pricing. To be safe, stick within the price range that your agent lays out for you.

Lastly, bear in mind that the price you paid for your house is no longer relevant – nor is the amount you've spent over the years on upkeep and repairs. All that matters is what comparable homes in your area are selling for *right now*.

4.   Why do homes sell above the asking price?

In our area, it is very common for homes to sell at a price higher than the original asking price listed by the seller. Buyers and sellers alike frequently ask their Realtors®: why is this the case? Why do sellers not ask for their homes what they actually expect to get? The answer is in fact relatively simple, and it all comes down to this: no seller or seller's agent can know for certain what a home will sell for; all they can do is ask for a price they deem realistic based on the prices of other comparable sold homes.

Here in the East Bay, we live adjacent to a populous, world-renowned city with great weather and outstanding amenities. Ours is a highly desirable area, but one with a limited supply of homes. Because there is not much space in which to build new housing, there is a shortage of newly available inventory on the market. Of course every market is different – this is likely not the case in many communities in the Midwest, for instance, where there is more inventory and thus less competition for housing. Our market, however, is extremely competitive. This is what can lead anxious buyers to offer more for a house than is asked – buyers will go above and beyond to secure a house in a coveted and finite market. (Of course, not all homes sell over the asking price, but many do.)

Our market is such that, before a home is listed, the seller and seller's agent will compare, or "comp," it to other homes that have recently been listed and sold. Because of the desirable location and limited local inventory, the home will likely generate interest among a large pool of potential buyers; this competition will lead the buyers to drive the price upward and commence a bidding war – in other words, to submit offers over the asking price. Depending on interest, the sale price of a home will climb, in effect, as the number of buyers who choose to write offers on the home increases. Each buyer hopes to outbid the others by coming up with the highest offer with the best terms. In the end, it is still a guessing game. Neither the seller nor the seller's agent can realistically anticipate the price a home may go to, since there is no way to know what sort of offer each buyer will write. All a seller can do is try to price his home competitively based on comps. The market will determine the final sale price based on the number of interested buyers and what each buyer offers; it is not in the seller's or agent's control.

One recent example is a home we listed on Bonita Avenue in Piedmont. Listed at $1,695,000, the home eventually sold for $2,110,000 due to heavy interest. We would never have listed the home at such a high price to start, because it would not have "comp'ed out" or compared realistically, at $2,110,000 (especially since it had only three bedrooms and no garage). Even though we knew it would be a popular house, there was no way to know just how much interest it would generate. Listing the home at $1,695,000 was a marketable price. A home in the Oakland Hills listed at $775,000 recently sold for $901,000. Of course no one knew where the bids would come in, but I am certain of one thing – the sellers were ecstatic! There is no rhyme or reason to the amount, or percentage over, a home will go. Take note: to be sure a seller does not lose an opportunity to generate interest, it cannot be emphasized enough just how invaluable it is to do all the preparation work recommended – which occurs prior to marketing the home or placing it on the market. Be sure your home is presented at its best—in any market.

It would be highly unwise for a seller and his agent to anticipate a bidding war if they list the home too high from the beginning. If you do this, potential buyers will assume that you actually expect them to bid even higher than that. No offers will come in if a home is priced too high; rather than make a lower offer, buyers will wait to make any offers only until after the seller brings the price down. It is therefore very important for you as the seller to generate some momentum first. When your home is priced accordingly, people will become interested and may decide to push their bids over the listed price. A home's final sale price depends on how many interested parties are writing offers at that time or presenting on your offer date. Not every home will sell insanely high and generate such a commotion, so all recent home sales must be taken into consideration. In short, all a seller can do is begin by pricing a home at a value that is realistic in comparison to other similar, recently sold homes. The rest depends on buyer enthusiasm and interest.

> On a separate but related note, it is useful for sellers to know that they are never obligated to accept any offer. Even if someone makes a full-price, non-contingent offer on your property, you are perfectly permitted to decline that offer. Many sellers then ask: if this is the case, am I still obligated to pay my agent's commission? The answer is no – despite the fact that your agent succeeded in securing you a full-price offer, you don't have to pay his or her commission if the sale is not finalized. An agent could try to fight for his or her commission in this circumstance, but it would be unlikely that the agent would win the dispute. Any offer is merely an invitation to make a deal; you are never obligated to accept.

5. How do I guarantee that my home makes a great first impression?

When preparing your home for market, initial impressions are critical. From the second that a potential buyer lays eyes on your home, he is already deciding whether or not he could see himself living there. Therefore, initial impressions are in some ways most important. If a first impression is spoiled, there will be no second chance.

Initial impressions of a home tend to come from two sources, the first being the Internet. Increasingly, potential buyers are beginning their house shopping online and, as such, their first perceptions of your home come from what they see on the Internet. Buyers will first judge your home based on its photos. These photos represent your one shot to make a great or enticing first impression. If they are unprofessional or low quality, the buyer loses interest and will not consider your home as a viable option. Furthermore, if the photos depict a house that has not been staged, buyers will wonder if there is something wrong with the property (read more about home staging in question number 6 below). A home for sale must be staged from head to toe; one can't afford to risk doing otherwise. **Staging** is such the norm at this time that buyers expect to see it; when they don't, they assume that they are therefore justified in making a low-ball offer on your home. They also assume the seller is in financial crisis, whether or not this is true; right or wrong, this is the image you are portraying if you decline to stage your home. According to About. com, over 90% of buyers look at homes that they found on the Internet. This means that many of your potential buyers are people browsing the Web. When people begin their home search online, your seller's agent won't have a chance to comment or to explain the unique characteristics of your home. Instead, the pictures will do all the talking. As such, if your online presence isn't impressive, buyers will have no incentive to visit your house in person. Reel your buyers in with a striking presence online – the photos you post have the ability to repel people or to attract them to your front doorstep.

The second source for a first impression is the exterior of your home itself. Also known as "**curb appeal**," the initial appearance of your property says a lot about its value and indicates to buyers whether it is worth it to step inside. If you want to sell your home, don't think that you don't first have to present it properly – you do! Here are some common suggestions to put your property's best foot forward: the home's exterior and its front door should be freshly painted to help it appear clean and bright. The front door is a great spot to make a good impression since buyers will be lingering here while the agent unlocks the door to your home or gives them the rundown of the property. Consider pressure washing the house, driveway, and any walkways. Trim trees and bushes in the front yard, fertilize the lawn, plant white flowers in the yard and lay down some fresh black mulch. Also be sure that all the windows shine. With the help of your agent and stager, it is your job to present your home so beautifully that buyers are eager to step inside. Your agent should have a team at the ready.

Profile of a Buyer

When you are in the midst of preparing your home for market—painting, carrying out minor renovations, planting flowers and, eventually, staging—it is important that you visualize your potential buyer.

For instance, in our experience, the typical buyers moving into Piedmont are parents in their 30s or 40s who have 2-3 children and are looking to move into the area in order to gain access to the exclusive Piedmont School District. Their most sought-after features in a home would likely include: at least 3 bedrooms on the same level (so all bedrooms should be staged as such), a level outdoor garden, minimal stairs, a garage with ample storage space, and close proximity to the center of town.

If you were selling a home in Piedmont with a sloped backyard or an abundance of stairs leading up to the entrance, then, you would have all the more reason to make your home shine with staging, landscaping, and other enhancements. Because it has become the norm in our market to present showcase-style homes on the market, anything less than this will be a detriment. You want your home to target a range of buyers and should seek to make it most appealing to all – this includes families, singles, younger people, older people, etc.

6. What are the advantages of home staging? Are there any staging tricks I should carry out on my own?

In the local East Bay market, professional home **staging** is *absolutely necessary* and worth its weight in gold. Staging is the norm nowadays in our local area, which means that the standards have been raised. No seller wants to distinguish his or her property as the one home in the neighborhood that has not been professionally staged. Furthermore, the benefits of staging have been proven nationally time and time again. For example, the National Association of Realtors® (NAR) has reported that the average staging investment costs between 1 and 3% of a given home's asking price, but generates a return of 8 to 10%. In other words, statistics maintain that after paying to hire a stager, you will make your money back, and then some, when your home sells. In addition, HomeGain.com found in 2011 that staged homes spend about 83% less time on the market than non-staged homes. Not only will home staging generate revenue for you, but also it will help you to finalize your sale quicker.

Staging is also beneficial to any seller because it works to present the home in the freshest, most aesthetically pleasing manner possible. Professional stagers are adept in bringing out a home's best attributes; they know how to use color, lighting, contemporary and fresh furnishings, and space to help you get the best possible price for your property. As the NAR announced, the price you pay to hire a stager will be returned to you multiple times over when your staged home sells for a higher final sales price.

When you hire a professional stager, you will likely be asked to move out of your home, completely vacating it inside. If you are renting out your home it is not usually necessary to remove your personal belongings before the property is shown. When you are selling your home, however, it is ideal—even imperative—that you empty the home and then relocate with your family during the marketing period of renovations and open houses. In some rare cases, stagers are able to incorporate certain furniture items or accessory pieces that you already own into their staging designs, but will ask that you depersonalize it by removing all photographs and personal items. The stager will create a checklist of furniture, artwork, and books to be removed – the less clutter and personal home furnishings the better. A stager's furnishings will typically be much more neutral, appealing to a broader clientele.

The goal of home staging is to allow the widest possible array of diverse buyers to truly "see themselves" living in your home. A stager seeks to make a home universally appealing to a broad range of tastes and living styles. Another benefit of staging is that staged homes tend to enter into contract sooner than un-staged homes, and seem to garner the most attention among buyers. You want your home to be the hot property that buyers are jumping to bid for. As an added bonus, having your home staged forces you to begin the process of sorting through your belongings prior to moving out. This will help you to be as organized as you can be once your house has sold.

Some sellers opt to stage or redecorate their homes on their own. While this option may seem simple enough, staging your entire house would require many hours of valuable time. Consider as well that professionals have access to many versatile furniture items and design accessories that you would otherwise have to purchase yourself. If instead you hire a professional, the work will get done like magic while you're running about attending to the many other responsibilities on your plate.

Ask your seller's agent for recommendations of reliable home stagers. In most cases, agents will refer one or two regular stagers with whom they frequently collaborate. It is ideal to work with one of the stagers from whom your agent will obtain bids on your behalf, as your agent will already have a good working relationship with those people. It is actually best that you choose a stager your agent works with as they have a history of working as a team; and as timelines often fluctuate, working with a flexible stager whom your agent knows is certainly more beneficial. If you bring in your own stager, your agent will not have had a chance to build a rapport, and it is doubtful that the stager will be quite as responsive as the agent's own stager would be. Timing is always imperative when preparing a home for market and issues inevitably arise; your agent needs to have comfort in knowing that she is partnering with someone who works as seamlessly, and who is equally as responsive, as she is herself. A great way to select a reputable stager is to view their work in other homes, online or in person. Your agent should easily be able to direct you.

Even after choosing to hire a professional stager, there are several steps your agent will recommend you complete prior to staging. For instance, painting the interior and exterior as needed, fertilizing your lawn and plants, having your windows washed inside and out, installing contemporary light fixtures and high wattage bulbs throughout your home, painting your front door, and cleaning your carpets. Everything in the home should be made to look fresh, spacious, and inviting.

In the pages that follow, you will find photographs of properties recently sold on our local market. Each of these homes was renovated and staged to perfection, in order to appeal to as many potential buyers as possible. Take a look at these properties before and after their mini makeovers to see for yourself – details really do make all the difference.

Preparing Your Home for Market

Inspections

When sellers are preparing their homes for market, there are many disparate threads to connect. Before a home can be staged or even priced, it must undergo a series of inspections. These inspections help determine what condition the home is in – whether it is in good condition, and ready for new owners, or whether it needs a few repairs before it is put on the market. The latter option is virtually always the case, since houses need regular touch-ups and all sellers want to present their home in its best light. Throughout the entire process of preparing the home, we are extremely hands-on – though many agents leave it up to the sellers to arrange for their own inspections, we will come into a home, assess it, book all pertinent inspections, and compile all of the inspectors' reports for our clients. We will show up for all inspection appointments so that we understand the inspectors' reports before we pass them on. Rather than leaving our clients to their own devices, we both prefer to be right there with them, helping to juggle these many appointments. Doing all this work upfront is rather like going to a check-up at the doctor's office: all the different components of the house must be inspected so that a treatment plan can be decided upon. With the many various inspectors' reports in front of us, we, along with our clients, will then sit down to determine what does and does not need to be done in order to get the home "market ready."

First off, sellers usually opt for a general pre-listing home inspection (see pages 106-8). Since the home inspector will most often suggest that we get a specialist in each field to come in and perform their own detailed inspections of specific systems in the home, we usually book all individual inspections ahead of time. Like the human body, a home has many different systems that work together to make it run. It is important that each of these systems is evaluated during the inspection process. After all, more items fixed means the house is in better working order;

and the better shape the house is in, the more potential bidders and higher potential buyers will bid for the home because you have given them less work to do. All sellers want to see buyers' bids go higher and higher, but this is dependent on the cleanliness and condition of the home. As the seller, you want to remove as many "unknowns" as possible so that potential buyers will be comfortable to bid high. As always, be sure to hire reputable service professionals to perform all repairs and inspections; this will also help buyers to feel confident about your home.

What are the various system-specific inspections that are typically carried out in our market?

1. **Structural** – Examines the foundation and drainage systems. Costs about $450-550 for the report. You most definitely want to pay for the written report because you will need to disclose the results of this inspection in your disclosure packet, so that buyers know what they're dealing with when they make an offer on your property.
2. **Termite** – This inspection will cover termite infestations, dry rot (often found behind stucco walls), windows damaged from rain or weathering, front porch leaks, garage wood damage, windowsills, French doors, etc. Examines the structure of the home, with the exception of the foundation itself. About $250-350.
3. **Roof** – If your roof may be at the end of its life, it's advisable to get a roof inspection. Costing about $120 (though we often get it done for free), this inspection is worth a lot to a buyer. Small improvements to the roofing can provide buyers with an additional 15+ years before they will need to attend to their roof at all. Having the roof inspected and then repaired, if necessary, will help your home be more appealing to buyers.

4. **Chimney** – Examines both the firebox and the chimney. A firebox may just need to be cleaned, but the inspector will check to see that it's safe to hold a fire and will look for any cracks (since, if there are

The Renovation & Home Staging Advantage
Charming Piedmont Storybook Traditional

Before   **After**

Exterior

Family Room

Kitchen

Staging a Home to Perfection
Elegant Piedmont Restoration

Before   **After**

Exterior – Renovations

Interior – Staging

Staging for a Contemporary Look
Formal Piedmont Estate

Before   **After**

Formal Living Room

Second Kitchen

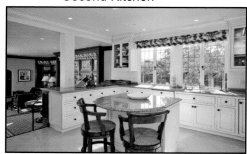 

Our goal was to create a less formal environment and a more contemporary look in order to appeal to today's buyers in their 30's, 40's, and 50's.

Grand Ballroom

Master Bedroom

Master Suite Office – Den

Pool-Level Family – Media Room

Bringing a Home to Life
Delightful Piedmont Traditional

Before   **After**

Dining Room

Kitchen

Living Room

Before

After

Family – Bonus Room

Bedroom One

Bedroom Two

cracks, a fire can start smoldering behind the walls of the home). The chimney could also be cracked, or, if it is too high off of the roof, it may need bracing. Inspectors might even recommend taking it down entirely if it could fall over in the event of an earthquake. They will also check for a damper, and a chimney cap. Fee approximately $150.

5. **Furnace** – For about $125, a furnace inspector will check the age and condition of the furnace. He will also be looking to see if the heat exchanger is cracked. If it is at the end of its life, he will provide a bid to replace.

6. **Water Heater** – Inspector will assess the age and condition, and will ensure that it is strapped properly, according to specified guidelines. Inspection costs about $125. If your water heater needs repairing, it may be best to replace it entirely, as this will only help you in the end – it could be around $800-$1200 to replace, which is relatively minimal in the scheme of things. This will be yet another feather in your cap for your home.

7. **Sewer Lateral** – This inspection is the newest local ordinance (research the East Bay Private Sewer Lateral Program online, and see the section on "Point of Sale Ordinances" below), and can either be addressed by the seller or passed on to the buyer. Sellers should get a bid (the inspection costs about $125; complimentary for our clients) – if your inspection is successful, you will provide the certificate proving this to your buyers. Otherwise you will disclose this to your buyers, sharing with them how much it will cost to replace, and leave it up to them (it usually costs between $4,000 and $8,000 to replace).

8. **Electrical** – This inspection is about $125, although we usually get it done for free. (When we refer our service providers enough times, it comes back to our clients in the form of free inspections. It's not a low-cost endeavor to prepare one's home for sale, so any complimentary services can be a welcome benefit.) An electrician will examine your exterior and interior panels, and any fuse boxes you

may have. He will provide a bid for any necessary repairs and/or a bid to upgrade service to your home, including the replacement of your electrical panel, as applicable. If there are small fix-it things to be done, do them – it will most likely be less expensive than you think. Plus, it will make a huge impact on the buyer, increasing the buyer's confidence level in your home.

Once you have paid for and overseen all these various inspections, you will receive bids from each service professional, detailing what needs to be done and how much each item would cost. It is then up to you and your agent to decide what repairs, replacements, or renovations to carry out, and what to defer.

With each inspection, the ultimate goals are safety and the alleviation of buyers' concerns. Sellers oftentimes worry that these home improvements will cost them $100,000 or more when, in reality, a series of small updates might cost them closer to $20,000. (Of course, this figure depends on the condition of each individual home and the care and maintenance of that home over the previous years.) Because you are seeking to mitigate any fears your buyers may have—so that these buyers will feel comfortable bidding higher—this investment may in fact be more than worth it for you in the end. Let your agent help you to decide what updates are necessary and what can be left to the new homeowners. In general, it is recommended that you take care of as many of the more

minimal maintenance items as you can – you can be certain that your future buyers would rather put their money into new bathrooms, a brand new kitchen, or hardwood floors than a new water heater or furnace.

As agents we are frequently asked why sellers need to bother performing this mini-makeover when the new owners will perform their own renovations to the home later on anyway. Aside from providing your buyers will some peace of mind and basic safety—both of which typically lead to higher bids from buyers—these updates ensure that your home is move-in ready. And this is where staging and presentation come in as well: once the systems in your home have been verified and updated, you can focus on the aesthetic features that make your home appealing to the widest number of potential buyers. After your inspections and repairs have been completed, your agent and stager will help to make your home look fresh and stylish to today's buyers. You want your home to appeal to the masses, and this is why you refinish floors, update light fixtures, remove old carpeting, paint kitchen cabinets, remove wallpaper, and more. You provide your new buyers with a neutral starting point from which to personalize the home and make it their own. The stager will be the last service professional to come in, followed by a professional photographer, and then it is time to move ahead to marketing the home.

Point of Sale Ordinances

Every state, city and county imposes its own point of sale ordinances. In the real estate world, "point of sale" refers to any rules enforced or assessments imposed on property at the time it is sold. In the East Bay Area, all properties (except for condominiums) in Emeryville, Oakland, Piedmont, Kensington, El Cerrito, and Richmond Annex are subject to the East Bay Private Sewer Lateral Program, which stipulates that

sewer lateral inspections be carried out before a property is sold. The cities of Alameda, Albany, and Berkeley operate their own separate programs, with differing requirements. To learn more about the ordinances of these and other Bay Area cities, please refer to www.bayeast.org/gov/ordinances.

The East Bay Private Sewer Lateral Program was recently established in response to a mandate from the United States Environmental Protection Agency, in hopes of preventing untreated waste from being released into the San Francisco Bay. The East Bay Municipal Utilities District (EBMUD) has left it up to individual homeowners to obtain a certificate from EBMUD (within 90 days after the close of escrow) proving that their sewer laterals are undamaged and are properly connected. If this is not the case and the certificate is not issued, the sewer lateral will need to be replaced by either the buyer or the seller as negotiated in the transaction. In our area, sellers often pass this responsibility on to the buyers. In our own recent experience, we discovered that our personal sewer lateral had been cracked for some time when it finally clogged and backed up into our basement. Needless to say, we had our sewer lateral replaced immediately. Sometimes you just can't wait!

Each city may impose additional point of sale ordinances. Piedmont, for instance, requires that a Sidewalk Inspection, costing $30, and a Permit History Search, costing $50, be performed on all properties at the time of sale. Consult your city's website to read up on the ordinances that pertain to your sale. In addition to the sewer lateral ordinance, sellers must also pay heed to local building permits pertaining to their city, and be sure to be in compliance with their codes. These codes include stipulations regarding the installation and placement of smoke and CO detectors, and the methods of bracing one's water heater. All such information can be found online, on the website dedicated to your specific city. Your agent should be able to guide you on these matters as well. (Costs and ordinances are always subject to change.)

Moving Matters

Estate Sales

After making the initial decision to move, your first question is likely to be: where do I start? It is normal for everything to feel very overwhelming. You will naturally be asking yourself where you will live during this procedure and what you will do with all of your personal belongings. To make the process as smooth as possible, it is useful to contact a seller's agent early on, ideally as soon as you have decided to move, even if it won't be for another year. It's never too early to gather information and become properly informed.

Though not all agents will do this, when representing sellers we like to start by bringing in an **estate sale** professional. This person's job is to help you sell or otherwise get rid of any possessions you do not wish to bring with you to your new residence. First you will decide what it is that you do wish to keep. These items will be placed in storage (read on below for helpful advice on organizing your stored items). Then, once your home has been cleared of everything that will follow you to your new residence, it is time to call upon the skills of the estate sale person. This individual will meet with you and your agent at your property and will move throughout the home assessing the value of all saleable furnishings. They will then go through and price every item according to its determined value. On a designated date, this person will hold an estate sale in your home. The earnings from the sale are split between the seller and the estate sale professional, who takes a certain percentage of the revenue. If you don't have enough items for an estate sale or do not wish to hold it in your home, some estate sales people will sell your items at local flea markets.

The major benefit of an estate sale is that you yourself do not need to deal with the items that are left over after the sale. Instead, the estate sale person will empty your home for you, either donating or disposing of whatever is left. You can opt to have your unsold possessions donated to a particular charity that you support, placed in a consignment sale, or given to any of your family members who may be interested in keeping them. Any charitable donations have the added benefit of being tax deductible.

In sum, it is helpful to begin with an estate sale because you may make a profit on unwanted items and will end up with an empty house. Though estate sales are especially beneficial to older couples who may be sizing down or moving into an assisted living facility, we recommend this route to any seller, as it is so much easier than going through the process alone. Plus, once the estate sale person takes your unwanted belongings away, you're done! Now your agent can get started on the long list and commence preparing your home for market – my personal favorite! But first...you need to pack what you're taking with you!

Storage, Packing and Labeling

Regardless of whether or not you choose to conduct an estate sale, if you are moving you will surely need to place many of your belongings in boxes. The task of packing up everything you own is a daunting one, but if you approach the process with an eye for organization, you will thank yourself later on.

First, most people choose to hire a moving service. It is useful to interview two or three moving companies before selecting the one that seems best for you. Also be sure to ask your agent for a list of reputable moving and storage companies. Don't underestimate the resources and referrals your agent can surely provide. Movers should provide you with the boxes you need, including larger wardrobe boxes. Alternative options also exist: the local Bay Area company ZippGo, for example, delivers plastic moving boxes that are easily stacked and transported, and require no tape. Regardless of what packing option you choose, organization is critical. Before beginning to fill the boxes, make sure to separate out the articles or furniture items that you plan to get rid of. You will want to begin purging as soon as possible – size down before packing rather than putting this off until after you have moved. Once this is done and you have narrowed down your possessions to those that you wish to keep, you can begin packing your boxes. Move through each room in the house one at a time – this will prevent you from getting scattered and will ensure that like belongings stay together in one place. The critical step is to label each box with a specific designation (i.e. Bathroom – Linens, Bathroom – Toiletries, Master – Bedding, Kids – Stuffed Animals, Kids – Board

Games). Keep all boxes corresponding to a given room in the same location, so that they can be unpacked all together. Once everything has been packed and labeled, it is time to decide how it will be stored while your move is in process.

If you are selling your home, you will likely have about a month during which you will be living in temporary lodgings outside your home and storing your possessions in a temporary storage space. If this is the case, you will need to decide if you want to rent a stationary storage unit for this period of time or if you prefer to rent a mobile storage pod that gets dropped off at your property, filled up, and taken away. Both of these options are equally viable depending on your preferences and needs. If, however, your new home is already set and ready for you to move in, you may have the option of simply filling your boxes and having your movers drop them at your next residence. If, like most sellers, you have yet to finalize the purchase of your next home, a rental storage unit is your best bet. Consider, when packing the unit, if you will need access to any of your boxes while you are living out of the house. If so, place these boxes nearest the storage unit's entrance.

Lastly, if you are in need of assistance in selecting a temporary residence for your family for the duration of your sale, talk with your agent to find out what he or she recommends. Many families live in a hotel or stay with family members for the time period, and others opt to rent another home. Have your agent help you put the word out if you are looking for a rental. Some families even manage to arrange a family vacation around the interim period of their move. Whatever you decide, do your best to remain organized and to live as lightly as you can. If your boxes and stored items are well ordered at the end of your move, the process of unpacking and moving into your new home will be infinitely easier.

Moving Checklist

Whether you are moving to or moving from your home, this checklist will help you feel prepared and confident.

Before Moving	Don't Forget
☐ Contact new and old insurance agents ☐ Notify friends, relatives, credit companies ☐ Change address with Post Office ☐ Transfer funds and arrange new banking ☐ Collect family records from doctors & dentists ☐ Collect school records for children ☐ Utilities & cable – transfer or cancel	☐ Defrost freezer and clean refrigerator ☐ Dispose of all combustibles and spray cans ☐ Plan special care for pets and plants ☐ Arrange for hotel accommodations ☐ Clean rugs and clothing prior to move ☐ Register children in school/activities ☐ Dry cleaning ☐ Prescription drugs
On Moving Day	**After Your Move**
☐ Plan entire day at new home ☐ Make a final check home is empty ☐ Give drivers current contact numbers ☐ Carry enough cash to cover moving costs ☐ Carry jewelry, valuables, and documents yourself ☐ Leave old keys for new owner/tenant ☐ Have meals for the day planned	☐ Double check phone and utility service ☐ Check pilot lights and hot water heater ☐ Have appliances inspected ☐ Change of address on driver's license, bills ☐ Register vehicles ☐ Check for needed home repairs ☐ Register kids in school/activities, if you haven't yet ☐ Prepare a home emergency plan

CHAPTER 6:
WORKING WITH AGENTS

The Role of an Agent

Since you will be spending many hours of your time working, collaborating, and meeting with your real estate agent, it is important that you understand what the role of a **Realtor®** is. Certain questions you may be asking yourself might include: what does an agent do? What does an agent *not* do? How do agents make money? Why should I trust a real estate professional? What makes a good agent? In our account of the role of a Realtor®, you will find answers to these questions and more and will come to appreciate the many hats an elite agent wears.

What does an agent do and not do?

- ❖ A top-notch Realtor® is fully on-call all the time, including weekends and evenings. Agents must be accessible by text, phone, and email. Aside from communicating constantly with clients, agents are often contacted by non-clients who simply wish to ask questions or seek advice.

- ❖ Real estate is a profession that keeps you very busy and gives you "homework" outside of the office workday. This job requires constantly interacting with new people and learning their stories – i.e. why is this family moving? What brought them to town?

- ❖ One benefit of real estate work is that it gives you control of your own schedule since, most often (as in our case), you don't have a boss to answer to. The job does involve some degree of pressure, though, since someone's future is in your hands and you don't get paid until you sell a home.

- ❖ It is hard work to start out as a brand new agent. There are so many agents out there that it can be difficult to distinguish yourself from the crowd and give potential clients a reason to choose you over others. It takes time and strenuous effort for a new agent to build credibility. But there is a bright side: each and every client connects with a different personality and a different agent. As a new agent, it just requires finding that client who gels with you and is willing to overlook your fewer years of experience.

❖ A major part of an agent's job is keeping on top of people. Multitasking at its finest! This involves confirming appointments, agreements, and meetings, ensuring follow-through, doing lots of fact checking, interfacing with contractors and service providers, and making sure deadlines are kept. The agent is the facilitator, meaning it's up to him or her to hold all the disparate threads together.

❖ Consequently, real estate agents—and myself especially—use every single spare moment in a day to contact clients and other professionals, to set up or shift appointments, to keep tabs on properties going up for sale or for rent, and to act as the intermediary between several different parties. Modern agents are constantly on the go and are constantly plugged into their phones, computers, and social media accounts.

❖ Realtors® also have to behave like therapists and guidance counselors at times. When buying or selling a home, people become worried and everyone wants his or her own way (i.e. sellers want to sell high and buyers want to buy low, and no one wants to be taken advantage of). Plus, many clients are misled from information they find on real estate websites that can't predict existing market conditions. It is the Realtor®'s job to keep all parties comfortable, informed, and appeased, and to talk them down from whatever falsehoods they may have read online. **Constant communication is key**.

> ### Contracts & Forms
>
> A primary benefit of working with a real estate agent is that he or she will equip you with all the paperwork necessary to completing your transaction. Without an agent's assistance, it would be all but impossible to navigate and decipher the numerous forms involved. These include purchase contracts (for buyers), listing contracts (for sellers), agency contracts, and the Real Estate Transfer Disclosure Statement, among so many others. A competent agent will thoroughly explain to you any and all contracts and documents before submitting them or requesting your signature. Should you wish to view the California Association of Realtors®' forms, please contact your agent. Aside from the C.A.R. forms, your agent will provide a host of regional forms as well as municipal disclosures. As you can see, it would be nearly impossible to be an effective buyer or seller without the assistance of a Realtor®.

How does an agent make money?

- ❖ Working as an agent requires working on straight commission, with no guaranteed salary. Many people would not be able to handle the stress that accompanies this lifestyle, since most people like stability where income is concerned. As an agent you never know what offers will come to fruition, if you'll get hired in any given month, or if a deal you've invested your time and money in for months will suddenly fall through.

- ❖ **Referral fees** help agents guarantee some revenue, and allow agents to continue to service their clients. When someone refers a client to us, we typically pay that agent a 25% referral fee as a way of thanking him or her. Likewise, when we refer a client to another agent, we will receive a 20-25% referral fee.

- ❖ Agents are only paid once a transaction closes and a home has sold. If we spend weeks or even months working with clients who then change their mind about moving and decide to stay put, we will not be paid a dime. It is important to remember that your agent will not be paid a commission until he or she gets the job done. If the home doesn't close, there is no commission earned and there will be no payment or compensation for all of the time spent working on the deal.

Why should I trust an agent to do a thorough job?

❖ Well-qualified, full-time agents work in real estate day in and day out. For us, this is not only our job but our lifestyle. In addition to our various certifications and training, real estate professionals know the housing market intimately and have experience negotiating a deal. Since Adam and I have been immersed in real estate for over 20 years each, we have experienced a variety of situations and have dealt with a host of issues throughout the years, navigating all types of markets. It is that experience, and the number of years spent in this business, that provide us with more to give to our clients.

❖ Strong agents often have a go-to pool of service professionals with whom they work each time they do business. They will frequently refer plumbers, stagers, carpet installers, electrical workers, lenders, movers, storage companies and others. When you hire an agent, you are securing an entire network of trusted professionals who have experience working together and will give you the best results because of their frequent collaboration.

❖ Also, top agents can be trusted to know their markets more thoroughly than any other source. Realtors® work nonstop and live within their local markets. A top Realtor® can begin to feel the market shifting within one day. You ask, how is this possible? Agents have their fingers on the pulse. When a market is beginning to slow down for example, suddenly agents will begin receiving emails from other agents who are all noticing that offers are not being made on their properties even after many disclosure packets have been sent out. Agents collaborate amongst themselves and feel when the market shifts, immediately. News and media sources won't reveal these day-to-day shifts until much later on. A top agent knows that, regardless of what a seller might expect his house to sell for, it's all about the market as it is now. Only a qualified agent will know how to read the current market – a website can never hope to compete. Each area is a market unto itself.

What makes a good agent?

- ❖ Aside from stellar communication skills, accessibility, integrity, and experience, a top agent is one who goes above and beyond.
- ❖ For instance, most agents don't choose to micromanage the entire buying or selling process. Home inspections and other reports are typically left to the clients to manage on their own. Adam and I, however, like to take a more personal approach. We help our clients by setting up and attending all appointments and inspections, and will verify ourselves that nothing is left outstanding.
- ❖ When representing buyers, we like to provide a special yet practical gift, at close of escrow. We usually give our buyers the gift of a home warranty for their first year of homeownership. This warranty, typically costing between $400-600, covers repairs to various home appliances and numerous systems, requiring only a small service charge whenever a repair is needed. We provide this service as a gift for the first year and then recommend that homebuyers purchase it themselves for each subsequent year, as it provides genuine peace of mind. The average agent may or may not want to spend an extra dime on a client to provide a service like this, as many believe they have already worked hard enough, but we run a business based entirely on customer service and personal referrals. To us, it only makes sense to go the extra mile because we value and care for each of our clients.
- ❖ A good agent is also a realistic agent, one who is careful not to over-promise when working with sellers. We are intentionally very conservative with our estimates; we never suggest an asking price to a seller unless we can back it up with concrete evidence. We always tell our sellers that what one can expect to get for a house depends on what's on the market (their competition) and which qualified buy-

ers are actively right now – not a month ago, not even a week ago. Many Realtors® purposefully list too high and then simply claim that "the market has spoken" when the house doesn't sell. In our opinion, agents should never speculate but should be realistic. Since we are personally invested in the success of each client, we treat them with honesty—and this is not always easy.

The Value of Exceeding Expectations

When selecting an agent to represent you, you don't want just a "good agent," you want an agent who will go above and beyond for you – one who will exceed your expectations at each and every turn. When your agent is hands-on in this way, you will be amazed at the results. The following unsolicited commentaries, taken from two of our recent seller clients, testify to the value of working with an agent who exceeds her basic responsibilities and leaves clients feeling confident, reassured, and gratified. This is how you want to feel at the end of your transaction!

❖ *"Thank you very much for all your help and attention on this project... You are definitely hands-on and that really does comfort us. Having someone coordinate contractors and make all the appointments really takes a lot of the pressure off of us. That to me is a specialty service, and I have to say I have not met a Realtor® yet that offers that service, until now! Just want to give you a very big THANK YOU!"* – The Galloway sisters (Christine Owen, Claudia Bliss, and Kathleen Mallernee)

❖ *"A brief, but most appreciative, note to thank you both for the exceptional job you did in representing us... You held our hands when that was necessary, you provided us with great contractors, you stayed on top of the inspectors and contractors, you didn't give us false hopes, and you provided us with a sale with a great price and remarkable terms. You were always available to answer our questions and we never got the sense that we were bothering you. What we most appreciate were the efforts you made behind the scenes to ensure that the inspections were carried out properly and how you stayed on the contractors to ensure that all uncertainties were either eliminated or properly documented. Your skillful negotiations with the various potential buyers and their agents probably netted us an additional $100,000 above the already over-asking offers we received. As you know, we have a lot of friends and acquaintances in the real estate industry from whom to select someone to represent us. We couldn't be happier with our decision to go with the two of you."*

The People a Realtor® Employs

One of the many hats worn by a Realtor® is that of a manager or supervisor. Realtors® are indispensable for their experience managing and working with countless professionals whose occupations carry over into the world of real estate. Without your agent's extensive list of professional contacts, cultivated over years of proven partnerships, you would be left to manage a diverse team of service providers all on your own. Consider the following catalog of the many people employed by a Realtor®; surely it will persuade you of the importance of working with an agent with experience in her market. In any given transaction, a real estate agent might employ:

❖ Foundation engineers
❖ Pest companies
❖ Home inspectors
❖ Plumbers
❖ Electricians
❖ Mold remediation companies
❖ Painters
❖ Handymen
❖ Landscapers
❖ Lenders
❖ Title Officers
❖ Storage companies
❖ Movers
❖ Website hosting companies
❖ Photographers
❖ Newspapers
❖ Magazines
❖ Advertisers
❖ Attorneys
❖ Stagers
❖ Housekeepers
❖ Gardeners
❖ And the list goes on...

Tips for a Smooth Partnership

Just as important as your agent's experience and know-how are her personal characteristics and sense of integrity. You want to find the agent who will not only get you the best deal but who will become a dependable neighbor and a trusted colleague for future transactions – someone you would feel comfortable referring to your parents, your siblings, or

> **Referrals**
>
> If you are moving out of the area, out of state, or even out of the country, ask your Realtor® or an agent you trust to refer you to a qualified and well reputed agent in your new location. Allow your agent to source out the best agent for you by utilizing his or her extensive network to find you just the right one. There is no need to go it alone or to seek out just anyone when your agent can advocate for you and be a great resource. All real estate agents are not created equal – your agent will be able to find you a stellar agent in your new market who is just as trustworthy. When we make a referral, we take pride in each and every one; we do not simply pass our client along to the first name we can find. We ask for local recommendations from people in our network, and personally contact each one to see if they will make a good fit for our client and to determine how responsive they are. We investigate each agent to find just the right match. We are also there to be a sounding board, to guide, and to answer questions during the process, while they are working with the agent we have referred. Referrals present a win-win situation for the client and for the agents involved, and should be taken advantage of whenever possible.

your best friends. By now you are aware of what qualities make for a stellar agent – but how can you yourself contribute constructively to the partnership? What makes a strong or exceptional client? Read on for some pointers on how to get the most out of your relationship with your real estate agent, and how to put your best foot forward as a client. This section will clarify, from an agent's perspective, what an agent expects and desires from the working relationship with his or her clients.

Both Buyers & Sellers

❖ Above all, a client should demonstrate his or her commitment to communicating and to being a serious competitor on the housing market.

❖ As a client, it is of the utmost importance that you learn to strike a balance between deferring to your agent's judgment and asserting your own voice. Our best clients are often those who give us full reign to do our job. If you understand that your agent is the professional, you will, for example, comply when he or she tells you that you need to remove certain light fixtures and stage your home a certain way. That being said, any strong agent knows that you, the client, are the one who calls the shots. The buyer makes the offers and the seller accepts or rejects them in the end – agents are simply there to guide and advise. So, if you feel strongly about something, speak up or ask a question! You should never feel pressured into signing or agreeing to anything. Your agent's primary job is to keep you comfortable and informed. Since communication is crucial in this relationship, practice knowing when to listen and when to speak up.

❖ Another aspect of successful communication is making your expectations for the relationship known. This means that if you want your agent to pick you up and drive you around to open houses, say so. If you are unhappy with some aspect of your agent's service, tell him or her. Oftentimes the agent may not even be aware, since buyers and sellers have different needs and wants. Set realistic goals and timeframes with your agent, and then keep communication open in the methods you agreed upon together so that you are both on the same page every step of the way. If your agent responds quickly and efficiently to all your queries, you should correspond with the same degree of respect and timeliness.

❖ Lastly, never be afraid to ask a question. You should never feel foolish asking your agent to explain a form or a procedure to you, since that is her job! A good agent would never ask you to sign a form before you fully understand it, and will be happy to share her knowledge with you. If you don't ask, she will assume you already know.

Buyers

❖ Agents love it when buyers come to them *first*. Some buyers wait until they've already begun the process before hiring an agent. At this point, they often have already begun working with mortgage brokers or lenders and may have started their house hunting online. While there is nothing inherently wrong with this, it is in your best interest to consult an agent first since he or she can refer you to trusted local lenders and can give you area-specific information that you won't find on the Web. Successful agents know that working with out-of-area or online lenders is always problematic – they know that you need a lender you can call or text immediately in an emergency, which more often than not, will be the case. Since buyers themselves don't pick up on these insights, it's best to begin with an agent who knows the drill and will guide you every step of the way.

❖ If you are a buyer, you also need to show your agent that you are a serious candidate in the financial sense, and must be honest with your timeline. An agent simply wants to work with you on your desired timeline, so it is only respectful that you share that information with him or her. An agent usually assumes you are serious about a purchase, and with that comes much of her time and energy. Serious buyers are preapproved for a loan (or are in the process of securing preapproval) and preferably do not have a property still waiting to be sold (or have the financing in place to hold onto both homes for a while). If you show you are serious by following the steps outlined by your agent, you will be notified about properties that fit your needs and desires as soon as they appear on the market. Above and beyond this, agents have other tools they can employ to find you a home, and we have ours; just ask us. Respect, commitment, and honesty are what a buyer expects and the same goes for what an agent wants –a solid partnership.

❖ Agents appreciate knowing that you are doing some of your own homework as well. Though it is the agent's job to keep on top of the market, it can never hurt for you as the client to be proactive in your own time. Double check all the information your agent gives you by verifying inspection reports, visiting your new neighborhood after hours, examining all disclosure packets thoroughly, and talking with neighbors and locals. Be active and visit potential properties on your own when possible. Serious agents love working with serious clients as it allows your agent the ability to best serve you.

❖ When it comes to securing a loan and then closing a deal, it pays to act promptly. Make sure you get all tax returns and other documentation to your lender on a timely basis so that he or she can get going on approving you for a loan. Once you receive a lender's preapproval letter, it's up to you to decide how much money you are willing to put down on a home. Keep in mind that closing periods likewise move quickly – in 20 years, we have never seen anything longer than a 30-day close. Because this is the case, you cannot make a purchase contingent on the sale of your previous residence in this fast-paced market. Your agent will appreciate your perception if you are able to realize this from the start and are flexible enough to keep up with the pace of our local transactions. Real estate transactions are proactive from beginning to end – your agent expects the same efficiency from you that she provides in her services to you. The market won't sit by and wait 24 hours for you to act or respond. It's all about opportunities in the here-and-now.

Sellers

❖ When it comes to working with sellers, there is one major piece of advice to heed that will make your relationship with your agent flow smoothly: disclose everything! It is without a doubt in a seller's best interest to disclose everything he knows about his house upfront. When we represent sellers, we sit down with the client and go over all the paperwork together to find out what condition the house is in and what repairs have been made. But remember, you are the homeowner – as agents, we are just beginning to get to know your home. We won't be able to best advise you if you do not paint us an accurate picture of the state of your property. To facilitate this, it's a good idea to carry a notebook around the house with you, jotting down repairs, installations, updates, and renovations you've made over the years as they come to your mind. Keep the notebook by your bedside. It can be so easy to leave out one or two repairs here and there, but these may prove important later. Disclose everything you possibly can!

CHAPTER 7:
Primary Financial and Tax Considerations

For obvious reasons, the financial concerns involved in a real estate transaction are often the aspects that weigh most heavily on any buyer's or seller's mind. Every buyer wants to buy for the lowest possible price, while every seller wants to sell for the highest possible price. The financial steps one must take to prepare to buy or to sell can also be very daunting – enough to discourage people from carrying out the undertaking at all. However, if one manages one's finances well and approaches the purchase or the sale with a certain amount of preparation, a real estate transaction can result in financial rewards for both buyer and seller – tax credits and deductions for the homeowner, and profits from the sale of the home for the seller. The ensuing chapter outlines what any buyer or seller should know in order to negotiate a financially successful real estate deal.

Financial Planning and Advice for Buyers

As is stated numerous times throughout this book, the purchase of a home is likely to be the single largest financial move you will ever make. As such, you simply cannot go about the process lightly. No one, no matter how financially secure, can purchase a home without some degree of preparation and financial planning. For starters, it should be commonsensical that, before buying a home, you should be debt-free with a fully stocked emergency fund. Once these conditions are met, it goes without saying that the most important financial aspect of a home purchase is the mortgage. However, there are several additional monetary factors to consider in the purchase of a new home.

❖ **CREDIT** – It is essential that you understand your credit history before you attempt to buy a home. The higher your credit score, the better your credit, and the likelier it is that you will be approved for a mortgage loan at a comfortable, low rate. Because of the lower interest rate, with a higher credit score you can potentially purchase a larger home. It therefore pays to go online and obtain your credit report early on in the process. After doing so you can correct any issues, set yourself a realistic benchmark, and work to improve your score. A trusted real estate professional can direct you to reliable loan officers and mortgage brokers, who in turn can advise you on credit-related matters.

❖ **PRE-APPROVAL** – After getting a handle on your credit, you can move forward in getting preapproved for a mortgage loan, with a letter from your loan officer proving that you can afford to buy a home and have sufficient financial backing. Some homebuyers are confused about the difference between preapproval and pre-qualification; preapproval is much more involved and concrete than pre-qualification, which is merely a loose estimate. As such, preapproval is standard and necessary in our market – in fact, one cannot make a viable offer to purchase a home in this area without preapproval. Preapproval is also useful because it details a specific loan amount that your lender has approved for you. More importantly, it means that the lender has received and reviewed your credit report, application and financials, including tax returns. This gives you a strong idea of the location and size of homes you can afford as it helps you hone in on properties in your price range. Once again, seek referrals from your real estate agent in order to find a trustworthy local lender.

❖ **DOWN PAYMENT & CLOSING COSTS** – Soon-to-be-homeowners must also consider the impact of the home's down payment and closing costs on their finances. Loans programs require a minimum down payment amount in order to secure the loan; this is typically around 20% of the home's price. Those who qualify might consider

Federal Housing Administration (FHA) loans, which require only 3.5% down. In addition, closing costs can amount to an additional 1-3% of the sales price of the home. Assistance is likewise available for those qualified, but should not be relied upon. (A buyer pursuing a FHA loan will not be competitive in a seller's market.) One component of the closing costs is the **city transfer tax**, which is customarily split equally between the buyer and seller. Piedmont, Oakland, and Berkeley all have a high city transfer tax, whereas most cities in Contra Costa County do not have a city transfer tax at all, but only a county transfer tax. And yes, Piedmont, Oakland, and Berkeley have that one too! To calculate your city transfer tax, you can visit www.DiMaggioAndBetta.com/City-Transfer-Tax. You may also wish to consult Appendix D at the back of this book, where we have included a sample Buyer's Net Sheet, detailing the total fees and expenditures incurred by a buyer on the purchase of a theoretical, $1,500,000 home.

❖ **MORTGAGE PAYMENTS** – Once you have bought your new home, keeping on top of your mortgage payments is essential. In addition to the monthly principal and interest payments, there are property taxes and homeowners' insurance to account for. If you are not the most competent budgeter, it may be wise to set up an escrow account to handle these payments so that they are paid monthly rather than yearly in a large lump sum. Homeowners must also keep in mind that unexpected expenditures arise continually – one can't forget to factor in the cost of repairs and upkeep, unforeseen emergencies, utilities, and living costs. Some financial analysts recommend the following trick: set aside 1% of your home's value annually for repairs. (We can guarantee unexpected emergencies! We recently dealt with the unexpected replacement of our very own sewer lateral. After all is said and done, I anticipate out-of-pocket expenses to total

$10,000, not including any damages to or loss of personal items, including our children's artwork and memory keepsakes.)

Tip: Owner's title insurance is a must – don't try to cut costs on one of the biggest investments of your life. Your mortgage lender will require you to purchase a lender's title insurance policy and, because so much can go wrong with title, it is worth it for you to purchase an owner's policy at the same time. (Both are customary policies in our market that obligate the title company to guarantee the transfer of clean title. The insurance prevents any unpaid liens or back taxes on the property.) Your agent should always check the box on your purchase contract noting that you, the buyer, want title insurance—both an owner's policy and a lender's policy. Once you close on your new home, you will want peace of mind. Life is full of surprises, so protect your investment.

INTERVIEW WITH A LENDER – ERIC LADRECH, CITIBANK

We interviewed Eric Ladrech, an experienced mortgage profession-al and Home Lending Officer at Citibank, to gain insights on the lending process from top to bottom. Should you wish to speak with Eric person-ally, please contact him at (925) 330-0201.

Q: As a lender, how do you qualify someone for a loan? How does the preapproval or pre-qualification process work, and what is the difference between the two?

A: *To get pre-qualified, clients will simply contact me and say they're thinking of buying. They tell me their income and how much they have to put down, and then ask me to calculate some numbers that will clarify what they can afford. Preapproval, on the other hand, is really going the distance. It requires clients to provide their income information and docu-mentation, including W2s and tax returns, and to have their assets verified for the down payment and closing costs. The information is sent to the Underwriter for review and approval. The Approval letter will be provided to the borrower. The last component used to satisfy a lender or bank is the appraisal. In this competitive market, pre-qualification simply doesn't cut it. One must be preapproved and have all one's ducks in a row.*

Q: What is the difference between working with a mortgage broker and working with a bank or direct lender?

A: *If a client doesn't have time to shop for a mortgage or has less than perfect credit, then a mortgage broker might be a good option. If a client has good credit, income, and assets, and is willing to invest a little time in the process, then a bank or direct lender would be the best option. If the client is willing to bring assets to the bank, he or she could end up with unbeatable pricing and a strong banking relationship that can pay benefits for years to come.*

Q: Why does it take some people longer than others to get preapproved?

A: *Once I receive a client's paystubs and W2s, the process is fairly straightforward so it's relatively easy to get the documents and issue their preapproval letter. However, some cases are more complicated. If a customer is self-employed with complex financials, for example, the process can require more time. In either case, having a client who is proactive and who delivers documents in a timely manner will always expedite the process.*

Q: What kinds of setbacks do you frequently come up against when working with clients?

A: *Sometimes the documentation I receive might not match up. For example, a borrower might tell me her income and then show me tax returns that don't support that income. That person can't get approved based on an income that isn't there. Other challenges include the property itself, and whether there are any issues with it, or if it receives a bad appraisal. It's important to affiliate yourself with a lender who is capable of dealing with problems all day long, because they will and do come up.*

Q: From your perspective, is it currently a better time to buy or to rent?

A: *At present, it is a great time to buy. Home values are going up! This is great news for the market but it's extremely competitive. With a shortage of properties on the market, and an abundance of people wanting to buy, getting your offer accepted will be a challenge. Only one person wins each time, and the other potential buyers have to keep on looking. I recently heard of a situation in which 30 people were sitting outside a property in Lafayette, waiting to submit an application to rent. It's very competitive and rents are also going up in this area. You might actually find yourself paying more in rent than what it would cost to buy. So, in short, if you can afford to own right now, you want to. There is always the chance for appreciation, meaning that over time the value of your home will tend to go up. Plus there is the mortgage interest and property tax deduction, which lower your tax liabilities. These are the two primary reasons to buy.*

Q: What makes someone a solid candidate for a loan? What can people do to prepare themselves if they're thinking of buying in the near future?

A: *If you're paying a lot in rental fees and have solid credit, income, and assets, as well as the desire to own your own home, then please don't hesitate to call me. My thirty years of experience can help you make home ownership a reality.*

If you wish to buy a home now but aren't yet qualified, I will work with you to create a plan that will put you on the path to home ownership.
It all starts with a phone call. I look forward to working with you.

Financial Planning and Advice for Sellers

It would be a mistake to presume that the majority of the financial considerations in real estate fall on the buyers' shoulders. Home sellers have their fair share of economic concerns to manage – in addition to the fact that most sellers become buyers once they move out of their original home. The primary financial matters that preoccupy home sellers include: 1) Investing in Home Improvements and Repairs, 2) Determining an Asking Price, 3) the Home Appraisal of Value and 4) Agent Commissions.

1.   Investing in Home Improvements and Repairs

As you will have learned from preceding chapters of this book, one of the most significant things a seller can do to prepare his or her home for market is to perform certain key renovations to the home. This step in readying the home for new owners can prove to be one of the most financially significant aspects of the real estate transaction for sellers— indeed, replacing fixtures, painting the interior and exterior, cleaning or replacing carpets, refinishing flooring, and cleaning windows can be costly undertakings. However, these repairs and cosmetic updates can make all the difference. Painting especially can be a seller's best investment.

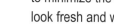

Be prepared to sit down with your Realtor® to discuss what improvements or touch-ups are strictly necessary and which are optional. Prioritize your choices and be sure that everything is within budget. You should never feel the need to embark on a huge remodel or to take out any new loans in order to sell your home – you don't want to take any actions that could negatively affect your credit score before you venture to buy your next home. Don't spend more than you can afford; your goal is not to update the home according to your own tastes, you are merely seeking to minimize the number of negative impressions and to make your home look fresh and widely appealing.

2. Determining an Asking Price

Another major monetary concern for home sellers is the asking, or listing, price of their home. The asking price is crucial, since setting it much too high will be detrimental to your ability to sell and will keep buyer's agents from showing your home. It is useful to bear in mind from the beginning that, though you and your agent will work together to set the asking price, ultimately it is the buyer(s) who determines the **selling price**. This is simply how things work. Heed your agent's insights (she will ask multiple qualified agents to confer with her on pricing as well), as long as she gives you figures on recent comparable sales to back up her suggested asking price. Rely on hard data and remember that the asking price is up to you in the end – not your agent. For a more detailed breakdown, head to Chapter 5 and see "How do I choose an optimal asking price for my home?" on page 108.

3. The Home Appraisal of Value

Many home sellers ask, "Should I get an appraisal to help determine my home's value? Is this a worthwhile investment?" The answer, in most cases, is that an appraisal is probably unnecessary. The bank conducting your future buyer's loan will conduct an appraisal of your home, but you yourself can rely on other resources to aid in selecting a fair price for your home. While appraisals are useful in some situations, **appraisers** and real estate agents define market value differently: appraisers look at past data while agents attempt to predict a future selling price. Agents base their estimates on past comparable sales, pending sales, current market conditions, the average time to close, the amount of available inventory—supply and demand—and many other factors. Therefore, for assistance in determining your home's fair market value, simply work alongside your real estate agent. Even if you have yet to hire a listing agent, most professional agents will provide this advice-based service for free, before being hired. Simply ask a trusted local agent for a Comparative Market Analysis, or CMA.

4. Agent Commissions

Understandably, a major concern for home sellers is the question of commissions and how they work. In almost all markets, the seller pays the commission of both agents involved in the transaction – the buyer's and the seller's. Most regions have an established or customary percentage that agents typically earn; you and your agent will negotiate this price together, though in our area each agent typically receives 2.5-3% of the sale price of the home. Oftentimes, a portion of an agent's commission is given as a cut to his or her company or brokerage. The agent typically pays marketing and advertising costs out of his or her commission. Advertising can sometimes go on for a longer period of time than expected, should the home not sell quickly. In most cases, the agent will assist with pre-inspections, will facilitate the prep and staging work, and will be present at open houses and more. For a listing or seller's agent in our market, quite a bit of the agent's time is spent on the preparation of the home and the pre-inspections. Then their work continues as the home is placed on the MLS and advertising and showings commence. And, finally, the agent manages offers and handles the entire transaction and the negotiation that inevitably takes place. For more on commissions, consult Chapter 3 and Chapter 6 of this text.

In addition to your agent's commission, you will pay certain other fees at the close of your sale. For instance, the city transfer tax is customarily split equally between the buyer and seller. To calculate your city transfer tax, you can visit www.DiMaggioAndBetta.com/City-Transfer-Tax. Additionally, the **county transfer tax** is typically paid in full by the seller, and can be located on the Alameda County Clerk-Recorder's Office website. For a more complete breakdown of the closing costs incurred by a seller, you may wish to consult Appendix E at the back of this book, where we have included a sample Seller's Net Sheet, detailing a seller's net proceeds on the sale of a theoretical, $1,500,000 home.

Tax Ramifications of Buying a Home

- ❖ Homeownership is accompanied by many tax credits and deductions. These apply only to personal residences, however, and exclude vacation homes, investment properties, and rental units, for example, which have their own set of positive/negative effects.

- ❖ Once you own a home, you can deduct property taxes and the interest you pay on your mortgage. These are deducted on Schedule A, Itemized Deductions. Taken together, they can add up to a significant amount. The most valuable tax deduction—especially for first-time homebuyers—is the **home mortgage interest tax** deduction. At the end of the year, your lender will provide you with Form 1098, which will delineate how much mortgage interest you've paid.

- ❖ As a homeowner you can itemize: the interest paid on your mortgage, property taxes, points paid to lower your interest rate, and some portions of the closing costs.

- ❖ **Points** are also tax deductible. "Points" on your mortgage are paid to the lender upon the execution of the loan in order to lower your interest rate. The rules governing how and when you can deduct points paid are tricky, however, and subject to many regulations.

❖ **Property taxes**, which can be significant, are likewise tax deductible. Property taxes are due twice a year in most cases, but it is helpful to set up an escrow account in order to pay these fees in smaller monthly increments, should budgeting not be your strong suit.

❖ If you have **private mortgage insurance**, this payment is also tax deductible. However, you are usually only required to have this insurance if your down payment is less than 20% of the purchase price of the new home. (This can vary from lender to lender.)

❖ While not all closing costs are deductible, certain items are deductible, such as property taxes and loan origination fees, which can be found within the escrow settlement.

❖ Many online calculators exist to assist you in the itemization process, but it is still advisable to consult a Certified Public Accountant who can help you to take advantage of every possible deduction. Your agent should not answer these queries.

❖ Lastly, keep the receipts from any major capital expenditures (i.e. repairs, construction, or remodeling), as these can be added to basis to reduce taxable gain when you eventually sell your home.

Tax Ramifications of Selling a Home

❖ Tax rules are unique in every state. Especially if you will be moving to a new state, discuss your sale with a tax professional who knows the specific tax rules for your area.

❖ When selling your home, **capital gain** refers to the difference between what you paid for your home and what you sold it for, minus the cost of any capital improvements (meaning any home improvements like kitchen remodels or add-ons that alter or improve the home).

❖ The **current tax rules**—pertaining to taxes owed on profits from the sale of one's home—are as follows: **married couples or co-owners** who file taxes jointly and who have lived in a home for two of the last five years may keep $500,000 in profits tax-free on the sale of that home. Anything above that amount is taxed at 20%. For **single homeowners**, the same rule applies except that they may keep $250,000. The exclusion of these profits—$500,000 for married couples and $250,000 for single owners—is known as a **capital gains tax exclusion**. One caveat is that the home in question cannot be a rental property. Consult an accountant, as there are several exceptions to this rule.

❖ If you made no profit on the sale of your home, you cannot deduct a loss on your taxes.

❖ Any gain above the exclusion level is subject to income tax, and is reported on the Capital Gains and Losses form (Schedule D). To reduce your tax, one tip is to calculate other expenditures into your basis, such as closing costs, capital improvements above and beyond standard maintenance, and the costs of additional assessments paid over the years.

❖ The either $250,000 or $500,000 tax exclusion can be used more than once in your lifetime, each time you sell a primary residence. This applies as long as you haven't taken the tax exclusion within the past two years for a different house.

❖ In short, you can sell a home every two years and keep the profits.

❖ These rules are continually being modified, so we encourage you to check your facts with a tax advisor.

CHAPTER 8:
MARKETING SELLS HOMES

From advertisements to For Sale Signs to websites to open houses, it is the marketing tactics employed by your real estate agent—with your help, of course—that will make the difference in getting your home sold. In this chapter, find out which approaches to marketing are essential and which may be a waste of your time. Make sure that both you and your agent are doing your utmost to put forth the best possible image of your home – if you're not, now is the time to amp up your methodology!

Executing Killer Marketing Techniques

When you are looking to sell your home, you need a seller's agent who is also a marketing master. The basic components of his or her marketing package—with which you should already be familiar thanks to your initial interview with your agent—should include the following elements, *at minimum*:

- A compelling description of your home, with professional photos and a virtual tour, on multiple websites
- Advertisements both online and in print
- A For Sale sign placed in your front yard
- A listing for your home in the MLS (Multiple Listing Service)
- One or more open houses (ongoing until the home sells)
- Postings on social media platforms such as Facebook, Instagram, Pinterest and Twitter
- Word of mouth – contacting local agents, brokers and neighbors to inform them that you're selling

Keep in mind that each of these elements is mere "surface marketing" – a way of covering all bases and reaching out to the widest array of potential buyers. The major behind-the-scenes work takes place when your agent markets your home to other agents, who then attempt to spark interest among their home-buying clients. Let us now take an in-depth look at each component of the seller's marketing strategy, with a special focus on how best to capitalize on each one.

Website:

In addition to posting written and visual descriptions of your home on his or her personal website and/or on the company website, your agent should consider it standard procedure to create a personalized website specific to your property. This exclusive website may use your home address as its URL (i.e. 451HamptonPiedmont.com), and should include lovely photos and unique details that truly distinguish your home from others on the market. The importance of professional, high-quality photos of both the interior and the exterior of the home cannot be overstressed. Buyers will be rightly skeptical of a home listing that contains either low-quality photographs or none at all. In addition, modern buyers love to see a photo tour of the property, which allows them to really get a feel for the home's layout. Lastly, the written description of your home that appears on the website must not be overlooked – the information you include should paint a clear picture of your home, while being both engaging and memorable. In addition, be sure that your home's personal website is easily accessible on a smartphone or tablet. Now that your agent has set up your property website, she next needs to push it out. A link is just a link until it has legs.

Advertisements:

Your real estate agent will post advertisements that promote your home in local newspapers, on the Internet, and in any additional local real estate magazines or publications. These ads may not be directly responsible for the eventual sale of your house, but they will help to generate an assemblage of interested homebuyers. Your agent might also send email blasts to fellow Realtors®, neighbors, and potential buyers. While detailed flyers and brochures were once the only effective means of advertising a home, to agents and buyers they no longer do as much to benefit the seller in today's high-tech world; flyers tend to get thrown away in favor of online announcements. Therefore, be sure that your home has a strong online presence.

For Sale sign:

If, as a home seller, you think that the good old-fashioned For Sale sign is an ineffective, rather inconvenient piece of plastic that only serves to cheapen your front yard, think again! For Sale signs are extremely useful in generating interest and phone calls. Your agent will order a sign to be displayed in front of your home, which identifies the agent him- or herself, the agent's company, and a contact phone number. It is critical that the phone number provided belongs to the agent or to an informed assistant who will be prepared to answer calls at any time. While it is certainly a powerful way for your agent to market herself and her company, the purpose of the For Sale sign is to generate phone calls from potential buyers and to simply notify neighbors that your home is on the market.

More often than you might imagine, a home is sold to a neighbor in your community or a local family who had always loved the house but never considered moving until they saw the For Sale sign in the yard. This occurrence happens at all price points – even multi-million dollar properties can be sold in this way. For this reason, it is essential that the For Sale sign is prominently displayed, so as to leave no stone unturned. You never know who may drive by your house unawares, admire the property, make an offer, and uproot their family and move on the spot! It has happened to us more than once. (Perhaps not exactly that swiftly, but the sales occurred because each buyer noticed the sign and/or attended the open house.)

Multiple Listing Service (MLS):

Of all the various tactics and resources used to market your home, the Multiple Listing Service, or MLS, is the most important. Any agent who is a member of the local MLS will enter the homes they have listed into this database, meaning that it has a wide audience of Realtors®. Once your property information is published on the MLS, thousands of agents will have access to it and can help you and your agent get the home sold to the right buyer. The MLS listing for your home will include general information (including the square footage and number of bedrooms), specific details (such as the existence of hardwood floors or bonus spaces), professional photographs, and any exclusive factors that make your home unique. A home will typically be entered into the MLS on a Wednesday, Thursday, or Friday such that the listing and photographs can populate the Internet before the weekend. Your home will generate considerable interest in the first few hours after it has been listed on the MLS. Buyer's agents will come by to preview the property and will then begin showing it to their clients – and this is what it takes to get your house sold.

Open House:

Soon after putting your home on the market, your seller's agent should be hosting an open house at your property. As you will know from reading the earlier chapter All About Selling, no home should be opened to the public before it has been staged. Home staging is no longer an option in the East Bay (as in many other markets), but is a mandatory and effective method of showing off your home to its best advantage. Review the sections on home staging (see pages 116-125) to be sure that you and your agent identify the best professional stager in town. Once your home has been decorated and staged, it is time to show it off to the world.

Open houses are a terrific way to bring in the buyer: they generate word of mouth and interest among the neighbors, and can also help your agent to attract future clients. Most often, open houses are held on Sunday afternoons and attract friends, neighbors, buyers, and other agents. The first open house you hold will likely draw in the largest crowd. In today's market, you will typically have offers a few days after the second Sunday open house, but if the house hasn't sold after the first one or two open houses your agent should continue to hold the home open the following Sunday and the next, until it sells. Contrary to what some agents may tell you, in our local market there are no drawbacks to continuing

to keep your home open; you need to keep the house open if you want people to see it! When a home is held open, you have a better chance of drawing in potential buyers. Plus, new buyers are coming into the market every day.

Before or after opening the home to buyers on Sundays, your agent will often choose to hold a broker open house, or broker tour, which in the East Bay typically occurs on Mondays and Thursdays. The **broker tour** opens your home to the Realtor® community. This allows agents to preview new properties just hitting the market, so they can inform their buyers of recent inventory. A seller's agent may consider offering snacks or hors-d'oeuvres to the agents, as an extra incentive to stop by the property. Your agent will be fully aware of the local protocol for broker tours, since each neighborhood has its own specified broker tour date and time. Piedmont and Crocker Highlands, for example, host their broker tours on Mondays from 10AM-1PM, while Rockridge and Montclair hold homes open on Thursdays between 10AM and 1PM. Generally a Sunday open house is set between 2PM and 4:30 or 5PM.

Keep in mind that the role of the seller in the open house process is simple: disappear! There is never any reason for the seller, the seller's pets, or the seller's children to be present while their home is open to

potential buyers – it is in your best interest to vacate the premises so that buyers don't approach you with difficult questions or put you in an uncomfortable position. Let them imagine themselves and their own families occupying the space – this will encourage buyers to connect to your home emotionally, without any distractions. More importantly, you as a seller may simply say too much. Sellers like to talk and buyers love to ask questions; if a buyer asks you a question you may answer in a way that scares off the buyer or causes confusion, and risk that the buyer misunderstands you. What you think is a harmless conversation may in fact have the opposite effect of alienating that buyer. There is also always the chance that you may offer up too much, perhaps making promises you cannot keep. To be safe, steer clear of your home at any time that it is being shown.

Social Media:

Given that today's buyers tend to begin their house hunting online, your agent should utilize his or her social media accounts, such as Facebook, Twitter and Instagram, to create postings pertaining to your home, perhaps providing the details of each open house or broker tour. Some agents opt to create Facebook advertisements for a minimal cost, which appear on the periphery of local Facebook users' homepages. These ads would provide a small picture of your home, its address, an eye-catching heading, and the basic information. Facebook ads are especially helpful because they allow you to target people of a specific age group in a specific geographic area.

To truly get the conversation started, your agent might wish to capture unique photos of your home, its staged decor, or manicured yard, and then post them to Instagram with an artistic filter. Because it is so simple and because most people are already frequent users of at least one social media account, there is no reason why your agent should neglect to market your home online and via social media. The best way to notify a large number of friends, neighbors, and colleagues about a property is to say so creatively on a variety of social media platforms, whether that may be Twitter, Instagram, Pinterest, Facebook, LinkedIn, Google+, or any other site. These sorts of social postings will be instrumental in encouraging the last—and perhaps most effective—marketing technique: word of mouth.

Word of Mouth:

Though it may seem overly simple, in some ways basic word of mouth advertising will prove your most invaluable resource. Your agent will speak to other Realtors® and brokers to alert them of the fact that your house will be on the market. These Realtors® will in turn describe your home to their clients. Early on in the process, your agent may announce your sale to your neighbors in the form of a printed postcard or letter, which allows them to help generate interest among their friends. You will contact your own friends, neighbors, colleagues, and family members to request that they help you spread the word. Your agent can also formally "pitch" your property to his or her clients during weekly office meetings, which most real estate offices continue to hold, or with a simple email to his or her other office affiliates with a link to the property website. You, too, can help sell your home. Any conversation you have about the sale of your home may result in connecting you with your future buyer, so never underestimate the power of real estate gossip!

CHAPTER 9: RED FLAGS

When to Be On Guard

Throughout the process of buying or selling a home, one may pick up on certain customs or rumors that seem somehow questionable or suspicious. It is always prudent to heed that inner voice that tells you when things don't seem quite right; this small voice may save you from falling into a trap or taking an action you later regret. Always defer to your agent and his or her industry knowledge before making a controversial choice, and be aware of the following sets of circumstances, which should represent red flags to you and your better judgment. From an agent's insider viewpoint, these situations should cause you to tread carefully.

For Buyers

Red Flags in a Home Description

As you begin your housing hunt, you will read over dozens upon dozens of **home descriptions.** Whether you find them in flyers, online, or in a local paper, you will probably find that home listings eventually begin to sound the same. As such, a questionable or incomplete description will jump out at you and give you pause; be wary of those listings that do not measure up to the standards you've come to expect from others.

For instance, it is a major red flag to come across a listing that provides few photos or none at all. In this case, it is very likely that there is something seriously wrong with the property. A listing should usually incorporate about twelve photos of the property, including pictures of any unique features (such as a swimming pool or a spectacular view) that are mentioned within the listing itself. If a listing contains no photos at all, potential buyers are certain to disregard the property altogether—and for good reason. If, on the other hand, a listing includes unrealistic photos or videos—ones that have been edited or touched up beyond what is reasonable—be aware that the sellers may be trying to deceive you. Since any photo can be touched up via Photoshop, a house or neighborhood may appear more attractive online than it is in reality. Always tour a property in person before making a judgment, or contact your agent for her opinion so as not to waste your time.

Buyers should likewise be wary of listings that contain excessively hyperbolic claims. Though these are exaggerations, expressions such as "Best property on the market!" or "Must buy now!" should produce feelings of doubt. When I read these phrases, the image of a used car salesman comes to mind. If you are a seller, be wary of an agent who describes your home in that way. It is natural for any agent to seek to market a property with persuasive and attractive language, but overblown, excessive wording is never warranted. A desirable property speaks for itself with its features and photographs, without over-the-top or absurd language to distract from the main event.

Thirdly, savvy buyers will be cautious of listings that boast a price that is too good to be true. Some aggressive agents opt to list very low, in hopes that they will inspire a bidding war and drive the price higher. Though this tactic can work, it can also backfire. Agents who price low walk a thin line and risk displeasing their sellers if the home doesn't sell with multiple offers. If you come across a listing that is priced low, it pays to be apprehensive and mindful. Check with your agent to learn why it is priced that way, as there may be a good reason. Again, rely on your agent to answer your questions, rather than spending your time making assumptions.

Lastly, certain terminology should be taken as a red flag for homebuyers. Phrases like "newly updated" may indicate that a house is a "flip." Be sure to have your home inspector check the quality and workmanship of the renovations. Another example is a listing that claims the home is "close to the center of town" or "easily accessible to freeways and public transportation." Is the home on a bus line? Is it within earshot of the freeway or across the street from the BART train? These terms are all relative – see for yourself what each term actually means to you! Here's another: "home office can be used as a third bedroom." Is the home office and/or bedroom in the basement? Is this "room" next to the garage, where potential fumes are a possibility? The list of misleading terms and phrases is endless.

On the flip side, some terminology may not be a red flag but may represent the honest truth. If a listing makes note that a home is being sold "as is," this usually means that the home is a "fixer" and that, if there are reports, they probably aren't favorable. A seller's agent should be careful of what they note in the MLS, as this expression can be a red flag to an appraiser, to whom it may indicate that major repairs are needed and the home's value may not add up to the price at which the buyer is in escrow. The home may have a large foundation or termite report, for example. (At the time I was writing this to you, I had just shown a home with a $130,000 termite report! This did not include all the other necessary repairs to the foundation, furnace, water heater, asbestos ducting, and the entire home itself, which was in need of a total remodel.) Remember that, once you print something in the MLS, it is open to the public – the MLS feeds to multiple websites for all to see. The buyer purchasing the home in question should know that their appraiser will read these notes in the MLS and will inquire about the reports. Should this happen, the home may not appraise at value. The appraiser will have to use the information in his or her report.

In general, use your best judgment when reading through home listings. Always confer with your agent, who will already be familiar with the properties for sale in your area; get her opinion so that you don't waste your time. The same goes for location: check the location of a property with your agent if you aren't sure, before getting too excited about the low price. Usually there is a reason behind it. The safety of the location is usually the number one reason why a home might look appealing on the Internet (good marketing!) but have a low price.

Red Flags in an Open House

As a homebuyer, after reading through numerous home descriptions, scanning photograph after photograph and home after home, you will also be touring through many open houses. When you do so, it is in your best interest that you look out for the following red flags.

First, notice whether or not many other homes within the neighborhood are also for sale. If so, there may be something going wrong in the area – talk to neighbors to find out about instances of break-ins, noise pollution, or other factors that may turn homeowners away. You can also check MegansLaw.com and talk to the local police department if you are particularly concerned about crime.

While touring the property, keep in mind that some home sellers can be sneaky in covering up maintenance issues. Always ask questions, read the disclosures, and seek professional advice from your agent. If need be, ask your agent to bring a contractor to the home and have it looked at more thoroughly – especially if the home appears to be in poor shape. Oftentimes you should do this prior to taking the steps to purchase a property. The home in question may be more work than you anticipated and are willing to take on. Certain maintenance red flags include: poor upkeep of the exterior or yard, chipped paint, bulges or cracks in the foundation or pavement, strange smells (which may be masked with excessive air freshener), doors that don't close properly, ceiling cracks or stains, and signs of pests. With your agent's help, you can always look to a property's disclosures to see if there was any serious damage to the home in the past. You may also opt to carry out a "clue report," which tells you if there were any insurance claims taken for water damage. If certain rooms are "off limits" during your tour, something problematic may be concealed inside. During a home inspection, every inch of the property should be open and accessible. If there are additions to the house, determine whether they blend in nicely or stick out in a conspicuous manner.

Take the opportunity to find out if the work was done with a permit, or done properly. The same goes for decks, which must be built to a certain code in order to meet safety standards. Not all work is done with a permit, but your inspector and/or contractor should be able to tell you whether or not the work was done properly. And, if it wasn't done properly, they can inform you as to the cost of repairing or improving the issue.

A home inspection is essential for any house you are considering buying. In a fast-moving seller's market, a seller may already provide an inspection report. If not, then your agent should make sure any inspections she arranges are thorough – order an overall home inspection, but also invest in specific inspectors who will examine the roof, chimney, fireplace, sewer lateral, furnace, and water heater, for example (review inspection protocol in Chapter 4). Rely on your agent to bring in the professionals and assemble the facts; your agent's cohort of industry contacts will perform their specific inspections and let you know how much it will cost to fix each individual item. Your agent will help to prioritize, and assist you in making sense of it all. It is imperative that you have this data before you make any serious decision about a home.

For Sellers

Eliminating Red Flags

When selling your home, you may not believe your home has any red flags. However, a potential buyer may think otherwise. You should take action to ensure that your property does not present any red flags to potential buyers. Be aware of the following items, which can turn off buyers, in order to put your home in the best possible position for sale – whether it's a buyer's or a seller's market. It is always a smart idea to put your best foot forward by presenting your home in its best light.

Buyers look for a well maintained home. Have your own pre-sale inspections done before you put your home on the market; this way you will know what you are working with and what needs to be addressed or updated. Keep thorough records of your maintenance history (including plumbing, mechanical, and electrical repairs), and decide what could use a touch-up. Your seller's agent can help you determine what repairs are necessary and should be considered before you sell your home.

Buyers also look to the surrounding neighborhood. Before pricing your home, consider what value a buyer would find in your area. Take an inventory of the local school system, the condition of neighboring properties on your street, environmental concerns (such as flooding, mold, contamination, or airplane routes), and the future of your neighborhood (its safety, economic prospects, proposed developments, local taxes, etc.). If you sense that your area might present certain red flags to buyers, be careful not to overprice your home. Once you overprice your home, the only thing left to do is to lower the price and follow it down. If you price your home correctly from the start, you have a much better chance of obtaining a higher price.

To eliminate as many red flags as possible, it is important that you are the expert on your own property. This means many things. First, you should know what information relating to your home and neighborhood is available online. Perform a quick Google search to see what photos and information potential buyers will find, and be prepared to address whatever is there. Make sure your agent is not using her iPhone to take photos of your home, but instead is using a professional to shoot several high-quality photographs good for both print and the web. Also, be familiar with the back-story on recently sold comparable homes; you want to be able to present friends, neighbors, and those determined to question you at cocktail parties with hard facts and local data. It is crucial that these interested parties get accurate information, as it is inevitable that they will share with others (including, quite possibly, potential buyers they may come into contact with). Many of the towns and neighborhoods we focus on are small communities unto themselves, where looking at homes is a hobby for many friends and neighbors; be sure you have the knowledge to dispel any inaccuracies or untruths. Word travels fast, and negative news even faster!

Lastly, be willing to disclose everything (within reason). Your agent will advise you on this matter, but it is important to be up-front about noisy neighbors, cracks in the ceiling, plumbing repairs, minor leakage, water in the basement, past issues and even nearby barking dogs. If you conceal some of this information, buyers might withdraw their offers later on. For that reason, it is usually best to err on the side of over-disclosure. Buyers will be less inclined to find red flags in your home if they see that you are making efforts to be honest and transparent. Take note: if you do get as far as the closing and then, a month or so later, your buyer learns of a break-in that occurred in your home or that your basement floods during the rainy season, and if for some reason you have not disclosed those items, be prepared – a lawsuit is on the horizon. Again: disclose, disclose, disclose, and disclose!

For Both Buyers & Sellers

Red Flags on the Internet

Both buyers and sellers should regard any information they find on-line with a skeptical eye. In real estate, as in life, it is never wise to believe everything you read or see on the Internet. Buyers may think that a home looks great online, only to find that the pictures were misleading once they visit the property in person. A home description may paint a rosy picture of the neighborhood that does not hold true in reality. Sellers may go online to estimate the value of their property only to find huge ranges that carry little weight within the specific confines of their market. In short, be cautious of online information and rely on an agent's guidance over and above whatever opinions and tips may be available on the Internet.

CHAPTER 10: CLOSING THE DEAL

The last leg of the journey begins right here! Once a seller's home has been listed and marketed effectively, and buyers have taken interest in the property, it's time to make and respond to offers and move toward the closing of the deal.

Buyers: Writing an Effective Offer

Understanding the Significance of Your Offer

Before we examine the offer-writing process, it is important that we stress the seriousness of any **offer** to purchase a home. When you make an offer to purchase, your action has the potential to determine how you will live the next years of your life, and how the seller will as well. Sellers will review any offer you make carefully and, if it is fair, will take it seriously. In light of this, our first piece of advice here is to avoid making frivolous or hasty decisions – in other words, don't make an offer if you don't really want to buy the house. This may seem commonsensical, but it's not uncommon for buyers to make spur-of-the-moment decisions when they allow themselves to get carried away with their emotions, or when they get caught up in a panic. For the sake of your finances and your future happiness, it is important to remain levelheaded and centered during the offer process. For one, your agent has a reputation to uphold – she works hard to maintain a reputation for making serious offers. In order for her to be a successful agent for you and for future clients, she must uphold this position. Secondly, you as a buyer will earn a reputation in the real estate community for being fickle if you do not follow through. Persistence and integrity are extremely important in this business. Word travels fast in small communities, amongst agents and even sellers.

Once you have grasped the significance of an offer, the next step is to understand how the offer-making process works in our local markets. While your buyer's agent is the one responsible for walking you through this process—from making the offer to obtaining a loan, and from inspections to insuring your new home—you yourself will want to be aware of what is going on every step of the way. If you are ever unclear, at any juncture, just ask.

Establishing a Price

Once a buyer has identified a desirable home, reviewed its disclosure packet, asked any questions he or she has and is comfortable with the answers, the buyer then works with the agent to establish the price they would like to offer. The buyer's agent will contact the seller's agent to get an idea of how many disclosure packets were sent out and how many other agents will be writing offers. Being aware of the "competition"—other buyers vying for the same house—helps an agent and her client to decide how competitive their offer needs to be. Though not everyone who requests a disclosure packet will necessarily make an offer on the house, the number of packets sent out is a good general estimate of how popular a home is to buyers. If it seems that there will be many offers made due to the popularity of the home, there is a greater potential for offers to be made above the asking price. In most cases, my client and I will wait to establish our **offer price** until the day of or the day before offers are due, as it is helpful to have the most accurate estimate of the number of other buyers writing on the property before choosing our final offer price. Choosing a fair and competitive price is very difficult since it is virtually a guessing game. No one, not even the seller's agent, will know what the offers will be until they are presented, one at a time.

It is important to act quickly once you decide to make an offer on a house you want. In our fast-paced market, you'll want to heed the advice of your agent so that you don't miss the offer deadline for a home. Your offer price is established based on the number of other confirmed offers and, often, many conversations between the buyer, the agent, and the buyer's lender about what maximum the buyer can possibly afford. (Note: When a buyer's agent confirms with the seller's agent that she will be presenting an offer on the offer date, this is called a confirmed offer). Other factors that will affect your stated offer include: the heat of the current market, the seller's time frame, how much interest has already been expressed about this property, whether this house is truly one-of-a-kind for you, and the price at which pending homes are closing. Ask your agent to gather some information on the sale prices of pending and recently sold homes, but not homes that closed three months ago. The more up-to-date data you can find, the better it will be for you. Even within a month's time, prices may have increased significantly. If your agent isn't privy to what pending homes will be closing at, you just may lose out. Up to date information is key to making a decision on what offer you will write. This is just another reason why your agent must be well connected and well liked by his or her colleagues. If your agent is not well respected, your chances of winning can very well be diminished.

Since it is likely that you won't get a second chance to increase your offer, you must put forth your best and highest-possible offer from the get-go. You will only get one chance to buy any given property you like, so this is the time to (reasonably) push it to the limit. While of course, no one wants to overpay for a home, in today's sizzling East Bay market, offering a price that is too low will most likely knock you out of the running for a home. Therefore, the local rule of thumb is to offer as much as you are willing and able to pay for a home, and not less. Ask yourself: what if I lost this home, and could have, would have, paid X? What is that number, the number that you could and would pay in order to prevail? That's your number.

Throughout the process of drafting your offer, imagine the seller's reaction to your stipulations and suggested price. Make sure your offer is both fair and friendly; there is no point in offending the seller and getting your offer rejected. Since this is just the beginning of the process of negotiations, it is helpful to put yourself in the seller's shoes to make sure that you are proposing things both you and he can happily agree to.

How do preemptive offers work? Should I make a preemptive offer?

Preemptive offers – offers made to purchase a property in advance of that property's specified offer date – are a common topic of interest among our buyer clients. As agents, we both strongly suggest that buyers think seriously before asking their agent to make a preemptive offer on their behalf. Your pre-emptive offer would likely be the first offer the sellers hear. Unless your offer knocks them off their feet, the sellers will probably decide to wait—rather than accepting it right off the bat—so that they have multiple offers to choose from. If your preemptive offer is less than satisfactory and is not accepted, therefore, this may put you at a disadvantage if you wish to resubmit your offer at the designated time. When you resubmit an offer, even if that offer is higher than the original, the sellers may view the offer unfavorably. In a small market like ours, reputations matter. Both your reputation as a buyer and your agent's reputation are constantly on the line. Fellow agents in our community will quickly learn who the serious buyers are and which buyers tend to back out or write weak offers. To be safe, it is best to write an offer only if you are 100% serious. If you are set on writing a preemptive offer and the seller's agent agrees to hear it, it is only worth your time and reputation if it is significantly higher than the asking price. Otherwise, the best advice is to simply wait for the offer date.

Components of an Offer to Purchase

Aside from the price you are proposing, your offer will include many other elements. The offer will stipulate how you intend to finance the home and what your down payment will be. It will also break down various closing costs involved in the sale. In our area it is customary that the buyer pays his or her own closing costs, and the seller pays his or her own closing costs. It may be useful to ask your agent for an estimate of the closing costs you will incur, based on a guesstimated offer price, so that you have a better idea of what you are committing to. Some fees in this region of California can seem lofty if you aren't familiar with them already; if you have purchased a home elsewhere, our closing costs may seem especially exorbitant.

In addition, your offer will outline what inspections will be performed, timetables (such as contingency periods, the **close of escrow** or COE— usually 14-21 days in a competitive market—and signing), terms of cancellation, when the buyer will receive physical possession of the home, how any potential disputes would be mediated, and whether any personal property will be included in the home purchase. (The inclusion of personal property in a sale almost never occurs in the East Bay.) As in every deal, it is in each person's interest to get the deal closed in a timely fashion, and in today's seller's market buyers are virtually never in the position to ask sellers to do anything above and beyond the norm; rather, the exact opposite is true. (Oftentimes, buyers will give the seller a free rent back, thereby allowing the seller to remain in possession of the home for a designated timeframe. Typical timeframes may be 3 days to 3 weeks after the close of escrow, though I have even heard of some cases in which buyers have given the sellers 3-4 months or even a year to remain in possession! It's a good tactic and a smart way to engage the seller.) Your agent will advise you on the appropriate length of time needed to close your deal; a typical closing for a sale is about 30 days, though an expedited closing has been known to happen in about 14 days. Your offer will—and must—contain a specific closing date, which gives both the buyer and the seller the freedom to make plans for moving. Any offer to purchase must also be accompanied by a preapproval letter, demonstrating that you are a serious candidate who is in a position to purchase and close on the home.

Lastly, we both like to have our buyer clients write personal letters to include in their offers. It is always good practice for a buyer making an offer on a home to prepare a personal letter to the sellers. These letters describe a bit about the buyers, their family lifestyle, and their background, so that the sellers feel acquainted with the people who may be moving into their home. Providing some personal information allows the seller to empathize and identify with you and your family (your family may mean you and your dog). You will not be presenting the letter yourself, but your agent will use it to open up the conversation with the seller's agent (hopefully with the seller present) when they hear your offer and read your letter. Sellers tend to truly appreciate this personal touch, and feel more confident selling their home to a family that really loves their home. Still, more often than not, price and terms will be what dictate an acceptance.

When writing a personal letter, paint a picture of your family and describe why you love the home you are offering on. A personal note may include why their home is special to you, what you like about the neighborhood, if you have friends or family nearby, and any other factors you feel are important to you. Sellers love to know who is buying their home and who will be caring for it over the next decade, or even longer. It is important to share a bit about yourselves, about your jobs, if you have children and/or any pets, plus anything else you want to share. Think of it as a love letter to the sellers about their home. We never know when a letter will help and make the difference, but we can say for sure—it will not hurt.

The most dramatic story we can share on this topic occurred when Adam presented an offer on behalf of his buyers for a home with multiple offers in the Upper Rockridge/Claremont Pines neighborhood of Oakland. Though he prevailed, this was not due to price or terms, but in fact, it was Adam's glowing presentation and the buyer's letter that won the home. Adam sold the home for $100,000 less than the highest offer. This is a true story. Now that is a story to remember! Do take note: though many buyers do this, it is not ethical to attach a photograph of you or your family with your offer and letter. It is in fact a HUD violation to submit photographs of clients with offers, as there is the potential for discrimination.

Contingencies

Your offer may contain contingencies, which are certain events that must occur within specific timeframes and prior to the close of escrow. When you include contingencies in your offer, this means that your offer to buy the house is contingent on certain elements. You might, for instance, say you will agree to follow through with buying the house only if the inspections are favorable to you, or if you succeed in selling your old house first. (It is highly unusual for a buyer to make an offer contingent on the sale of their current home, as this contingency would make your offer weak and you, an uncompetitive buyer, since the seller will not wish to wait around for your own sale to go through). If these contingencies are not attended to and you do not wish to remove them by signing off on the Contingency Removal Form, you as the buyer are allowed to cancel the deal and get your deposit money back, as long as you are within the contingency period. Prior to canceling the deal, however, you and your agent may want to attempt to negotiate for a credit. Most of the time, this works

out. Once the contingencies have been removed, however, if you then have a change of heart and decide to back out of the deal your deposit may be forfeited to the seller. Speak to your agent if you would like to know more about lost deposits. As in all legal matters, situations will vary.

When possible, and when a buyer feels very confident, he or she may opt to go **non-contingent** on some or all of the specified contingencies. For example, the Loan Contingency allots time for the lender to gain final loan approval. But if a buyer is in a strong financial position, the buyer and the buyer's agent might opt to go non-contingent on Loan and/or Appraisal, marking Zero (0) Days on the offer form. If a buyer cannot be non-contingent on this particular contingency, 7-10 days are often

allotted to complete this contingency. This time period is determined by the buyer's lender, who will provide a comfort level for the buyers based on their finances. Though Adam and I try to keep our contingencies as short and as competitive as possible—so that the seller will either sign or counter our offers—agents who are unfamiliar with our local market or who are simply uncompetitive will default to the standard 17-day time period. Ideally, we prefer to write an offer with Zero (0) Days or no Loan contingency. But in every case, the buyers must be comfortable removing that contingency based on the confidence level that the lender has provided them with, both verbally and in the form of the preapproval letter.

The next contingency is the Appraisal Contingency, which grants time to complete a home appraisal. Depending on the borrower, our typical contingency period for an appraisal is either non-contingent (0) or 7-10 days. A borrower may feel comfortable without an appraisal contingency, or may not. Once again, it depends on the borrower's financial picture and his or her willingness to bring a higher down payment to close the escrow, should the home not appraise. Many buyers purchasing higher-end homes don't mind this, as they are already putting a substantial amount of money into the property along with a small loan, so if a home didn't appraise it wouldn't jeopardize the deal. Some buyers, however, need an Appraisal Contingency as they are putting the minimum down payment into a property; for them, if a home doesn't appraise they will need to bring more money into the deal if they can or, if not, the Appraisal Contingency allows them to walk away and get their deposit money back. A bank will loan up to 80% of the appraised value. Neither of us has ever had an issue with a home not appraising, either when representing a buyer or a seller. But as agents we are obligated to illustrate all possible scenarios and walk our clients through all potential "what if" situations—it is all about buyer confidence and comfort. We also encourage frequent communication with a buyer's lender to help set buyers at ease. Prior to presenting our buyer's offer, we speak directly with their lender to make sure he is satisfied so that we can present an offer on the buyer's behalf with confidence. As agents, we both work tirelessly to protect our clients, ensure that they don't get stuck in a tricky situation, and are informed and comfortable at all times.

On the subject of lenders, it is imperative a lender understands the agent's role. If a lender does not communicate with us, this is a red flag. A lender may work with buyers in a wide range of markets and areas, but agents more often specialize. The agent is going to be the one providing information to both the buyer and the lender on our local customs and, more often than not, the agent will be the one translating information to her buyers that may seem overwhelming or is simply new territory. It is of utmost importance, then, that the lender communicates regularly with the agent so that the agent can be on top of the transaction in case any unforeseen issues arise. It is also the buyer's agent who is in constant communication with the seller's agent in order to keep him or her informed, happy, and calm. Again, working as a team is a must in any transaction.

The final contingency is the Physical, or Home Inspection Contingency. With this contingency, a buyer can inspect anything related to the property. Though this rarely happens, a buyer can theoretically request a cancellation of contract and receive the full deposit back, should anything appear unsuitable in the inspection reports. Buyers who are comfortable with what they have read in the disclosure packet can choose to write non-contingent in regards to the home inspection. If, however, a buyer is unsure or is a first-time homebuyer, then we will include a 3-to-5-day Home Inspection Contingency. While some agents will write in a 7-to-10-day Home Inspection Contingency, shorter contingency periods present a more competitive offer and still provide more than enough time to get the job done—of course, if the agent has strong relationships with her contractors and service providers as we do.

What does it mean if a buyer is non-contingent? A buyer would choose to be non-contingent if the homeowner has provided enough information on the home to make the buyer comfortable and fully knowledgeable about the home. In the homeowner's thorough disclosure packet, a buyer will find the area standard forms plus a termite report, a general home inspection report, and perhaps individual receipts for any completed work or inspection reports detailing the cost of repairs to a variety of systems, including the sewer lateral, furnace, water heater, chimney, fireplace, roof, electrical and foundation. Sometimes, if a buyer is extremely interested in a home and is prepared to bid high, we will request permission from the seller's agent if we can pre-inspect a home. If a buyer is very serious, wants to present a non-contingent offer, and doesn't mind incurring the cost of the inspection—ranging from $450-$700—this is oftentimes a good way to go.

Finally, once all the terms are in place, we will draw up the offer and have the buyer(s) sign the offer. With advanced technology, a program called DocuSign® (adopted by many attorneys as well) allows buyers to sign the offer even while in different parts of the country, or just down the street, while at dinner, or at their child's lacrosse game. The agent simply uploads the offer and sends it to the buyers. Via DocuSign®, the buyers can then read and sign the document electronically. The agent receives the signed copy back in her own email inbox – it's a pain-free process with no wet signatures required. After signing their offer, a preapproval letter is requested from the lender or mortgage broker designating the buyer's offer price, no more or no less as to not show the buyer's hand. The preapproval letter, the offer, and the buyer's "love letter" complete the offer package.

Loss of Deposit

Buyers who are unsure of how to maneuver through their offer and/or their purchase contract should always ask questions. Agents are so familiar with the process that they may assume you are as well. All questions are good questions, and are never bothersome.

When buyers have a contingency in their offer, they are protected by that specified timeline. Buyers will not forfeit their deposit should they choose to cancel the contract in writing, so long as they do so on or before the date that their contingency is due. Buyers can choose to remove their contingencies, whether they have a loan, appraisal, and/or home inspection contingency. They can also request an extension if necessary. A few examples of reasons one may choose to extend include: 1) If the appraisal did not get turned in to the lender in a timely manner; 2) If the lender needs more time to underwrite the loan, or; 3) If the buyers need to perform further inspections and their agent is unable to get appointments in the necessary time frame. Lastly, buyers can choose to negotiate their findings with the seller – though, of course, the agents will do this on behalf of the buyer and the seller. Sometimes the seller will concede a full credit or a partial credit, or they may choose not to offer any credit. At this time, the buyers make their decision to remove their contingency and move forward, or to cancel the contract. Your agent will keep you informed regarding your contingency periods and timelines, so rest assured that you should not forfeit a deposit as long as you and your agent are in constant communication and are following the terms as outlined in your ratified offer.

Presenting the Offer

A good and thorough buyer's agent will make an appointment with the seller's agent to present their client's offer in person. It is customary in our market that a buyer's agent presents her offer to the sellers and the seller's agent at one time; usually appointments are scheduled one after the other. (Not all agents take the time to present in person, but we believe it is important. We believe that any agent should take the time to build a rapport and paint a picture of their buyer(s) that may appeal to the sellers, as this may prove helpful.) Buyer's agents will provide a brief description of their buyer(s) and then review the terms of their offer, emphasizing the buyer's preapproval letter and encouraging the seller's agent to contact the lender should they have any questions. After reviewing the offer—including offer price, contingency periods (if any), and Close of Escrow—the buyer's agent asks if any questions remain. Ideally the buyer(s) will have signed the disclosures, accepting the contents in the disclosure packet. Many of the other items in the contract are what we call "customary," and the agents will review those as well.

When it comes to selecting a **title company**, many agents already have a preference as to which title officer they wish to work with. We have both personally formed a strong working relationship with a title officer at First American Title Company, and tend to refer our clients there. When we list a home for sale, one of the first things we do is open a pre-escrow with the title company and order a preliminary title report on the property. We usually ask that the buyer(s) agree to work with our chosen title company – although we cannot dictate, we can ask. Since we have already ordered and received the preliminary title report prior to hearing offers, it certainly assists in speeding things up if the buyer agrees to work with our title company. The buyer's lender will need a copy of the preliminary title report as well, so having it ordered in advance is helpful, especially to meet a quick close. As an agent representing a buyer, we suggest it is always best to be agreeable when possible, since the buyer and buyer's agent are seeking to get the upper hand so that the seller will accept their offer or draft a counteroffer, if necessary. Buyers should choose to make it easy for the sellers when trying to prevail in a multiple-offer situation.

Is Cash Always King?

When it comes to purchasing a home, many buyers think paying with cash will always constitute a superior offer. It is often true that, if a buyer is able to pay "all cash" for a home, the seller finds this offer more attractive since it doesn't hinge on loan approval. Of course, this is not the case if the offer is lower than the others. Those who are able to offer to pay in cash might think doing so is an excuse to give a lower offer, since paying in cash supposedly makes the offer more desirable. But this is in fact a fallacy; no discounts will be given for cash offers, and cash offers must still be competitive offers. In our market, cash is not always king; paying in cash is certainly not necessary to have your offer accepted. As long as a buyer has been preapproved, he or she is in a good position to have a strong offer accepted.

What Comes Next?

After making an offer, what follows? If your offer is accepted, you will then make a **good faith deposit**, also known as an "earnest money deposit," into an escrow account. In our area, this deposit is typically 3% of the purchase price; within three days, it is deposited to the title or **escrow company** that is designated on the contract. The title or escrow company is the neutral third party that holds onto the money while the deal is in the process of being finalized. Your deposit goes toward your purchase price, and remains in the escrow account until Close of Escrow (COE). Roughly 3% of the price, —though within 1-10% of the price in other markets—the good faith deposit should be large enough to demonstrate your seriousness to the seller. However, it should not be so large that it requires you to put overly significant funds at risk, in case the offer falls through for some unforeseen reason. However, bear in mind that the decision to offer more money upfront as part of the deposit may encourage a seller to accept your offer over others he or she has received. Your deposit is credited to the purchase price, and remains in escrow (cashed), until the bank funds your loan. Your initial deposit will be reflected in your closing statement as a credit towards the purchase price.

Now is the time to verify the terms of your mortgage with your mortgage broker or lender, and to begin looking into homeowners' insurance policies. In addition, your agent needs to make sure you fulfill all of your contractual obligations in a timely manner, as is stipulated in your contract. Your agent will ensure that your good faith deposit is submitted to the title company on time, with verification sent to the seller's agent. A few days before the closing, your agent will make sure you receive your **HUD Settlement Statement**; go over it meticulously, as it includes all the fees you will incur at closing time. These fees include, but are not limited to, lender fees, pro-rated property taxes, transfer taxes, notary fees, and the like. Your agent should facilitate an appointment with the title officer, with whom you will meet to sign closing papers, a.k.a. loan documents.

Note: If necessary, an agent can also arrange for a **power of attorney** with the title company, which permits one spouse to sign documents on behalf of the other spouse who cannot be physically present for the closing. This is often useful, as lenders will not accept signatures via DocuSign® and only accept wet signatures.

These closing documents are from your lender. The seller will not be present and nor will the seller's agent. (However, we like to accompany our clients—both our buyers and our sellers—to their signings, simply to provide moral support and to relish in their excitement. Remember, all this is fairly new and a bit nerve-wracking for someone who has never purchased a home before or who hasn't sold a home in 40 years. Our presence simply gives them peace of mind, knowing we are there, and should they have any questions.) When your closing date rolls around, a few days later, the process is simple: your agent will simply receive a phone call from the title company stating that the transfer of property is now on record. This means that you have signed your loan documents, the balance of your down payment was successfully wired to the title company, all paperwork is in order, and the loan is fully approved and funded by the bank. At this point, congratulations are in order – all that's left is to pick up the keys to your new home!

In some cases, buyers will choose to perform a final walkthrough prior to the close to verify that the home is in the same condition it was in when their offer was ratified. But oftentimes this walkthrough is redundant and unnecessary, since the buyers have already been spending so much time in the house and the escrow period is so short.

In-House Offers

Buyers frequently ask us about in-house offers. They worry that, if a house is listed with an agent from Company X, and an offer comes in from a potential buyer also represented by an agent from Company X, that buyer will receive preferential treatment and will automatically have his or her offer accepted. Luckily this is not the case, since there is no benefit, financial or otherwise, to selling an in-house offer. The real estate company in question will not receive more money, so there is no incentive to accept an offer simply because it comes from an agent in your agent's same company. It is highly unethical if a company were to play favorites. Whichever buyer makes the best, most competitive offer will most often get the home. It also helps for an agent to present their buyers' offer in person in front of the sellers, and not just the seller's agent, so that the buyer's agent can paint the most accurate picture of their buyers and can answer any questions the sellers may have.

Sellers: Responding to an Offer

Option 1: Accepting the Offer

Hearing offers to purchase your home will be a very gratifying and exciting experience. After all the hard work that went into marketing your home and preparing it for sale, it is finally time to close the deal and transfer your property to the most qualified buyer. Most contracts do not grant you much time to determine how to respond to an offer, however. While some agents allow you up to 48 hours to deliberate, we recommend making a decision by the end of the day. If the offer is not resolved promptly, buyers begin to worry that you are "shopping" their offer; in other words, that you are waiting around for higher bids at their expense. To be most fair and accommodating to all potential buyers, regard each offer separately and give each one due consideration. In this market, it is customary that you will hear all offers in one day, within a designated timeframe. Once you have heard them all, it is up to you and your agent to review the offers on that day and, ideally, to provide an answer to each potential buyer before the day is over, as is realistic.

When you have all the anticipated offers before you, you and your agent will read over each potential buyer's stipulated terms. This includes their offer price, loan details, down payment, any contingencies, and close of escrow. If you find an offer that is perfectly reasonable as it is—one that you are prepared to accept at face value—you can accept it immediately by signing it, and then your agent will alert the other buyers' agents that you have decided to take another offer. Whether by email or by phone, it is always a nice idea if your agent reaches out to the other agents to thank them personally for their offers. Adam and I make every effort to do this when possible. As soon as you have signed the buyer's contract, your agent has delivered it to the buyer's agent, the buyer's agent has initialed it and delivered receipt of the signed offer back to your agent, you have a ratified offer. The buyers may then move ahead with their inspections, in what is known as the "**due diligence period**." This is also when the buyers will secure financing and begin addressing any and all contingencies, until it is time to close. If none of the offers you receive are entirely perfect, however, you may wish to make a **counteroffer**.

Option 2: Countering the Offer

Perhaps you have identified the best offer, but have certain qualms about it or wish to negotiate a bit before accepting. In this case, you can decide to counter the offer. In a counteroffer, you, the seller, will outline what is acceptable to you regarding what terms you desire. A counteroffer isn't binding until the buyer agrees, but you can put your requests out there. You can even provide a verbal counter: the advantage to a verbal, rather than written, counteroffer is that it expedites the process. You want to ensure that your buyer remains engaged, as it is best to wrap up the transaction quickly; if you deliberate slowly, a more appealing property may come on the market and divert their attention away from your own.

 In any case, it remains imperative that you respond quickly. Doing so has the upside of setting the tone for your buyer to act accordingly; when you set a precedent for prompt responses, he or she will feel inclined to return the favor. This also puts you in control of the negotiation and sets the right tone to move the deal forward in a timely fashion. Furthermore, if you don't respond quickly, offers can be pulled while you are "sleeping on it." Until a contract is ratified, buyers have every right to back out and withdraw their offers.

If you have made the choice to counter an offer, it is important that you know exactly what it is you wish to propose. Your counteroffer will state that you, the seller, accept the buyer's offer "subject to" the following set of terms. Counteroffers typically request: a higher purchase price or a higher deposit, fewer contingencies or less time granted to complete them, changing the title company, or changing the closing date, among other proposals. As there is no limit to the number of counters that can circulate back and forth between you and your buyer (since your buyer can in turn propose changes to your counteroffer), you may be required to undergo multiple rounds of back-and-forth negotiations. Still, the two agents can usually finalize a contract quite quickly, with just a few phone calls between them. And once this is done, all that is left is for the buyers to work on removing their contingencies.

Option 3: Rejecting An Offer

The last course of action one may choose in response to a given offer is to reject that offer. All offers must be acknowledged and treated seriously, as they represent a serious petition on behalf of an interested potential buyer. It is important that you recognize that you are never obligated to accept any offer, no matter how attractive it may seem. Rejecting an offer should never make you feel remorseful. An offer price or listing price merely represents an invitation to make a deal and, while you must treat each offer with respect and consideration, you by no means need to accept one – even if an offer is a full-price, non-contingent offer. It is fully within a seller's rights to deliberate over the offers that come in and then decide not to accept any at all. If a seller does choose this route, he or she is not obligated to pay the agent's commission, as the deal did not close. It is certainly not unheard of for sellers to change their minds about moving, or to decide to wait to sell until they feel more ready or find just the right buyers. Should you find yourself in this position, simply alert your agent as soon as you have made up your mind.

Conclusion

In the desirable communities and fast-paced markets of the San Francisco East Bay, real estate transactions occur unlike anywhere else. The micro-markets of Piedmont, Berkeley, and the Oakland Hills all operate based on specific idiosyncrasies and local conventions, making it imperative that buyers and sellers alike benefit from the insider knowledge and wholehearted dedication of an experienced local agent. For this reason, we chose to compose this extremely localized guidebook and offer it to our clients, friends, colleagues, and fellow real estate enthusiasts living in and around the East Bay. Our local insights, spread throughout each and every chapter of this book, are based on over 20 years each of experience and success. If the East Bay has been or will be the place you call home, we believe that our guidebook will remain an invaluable resource for you and your family for years to come.

While this East Bay guide has undoubtedly been written for a specific audience and market, we have endeavored equally intently to compile the vast extent of our common industry knowledge, such that the book may be both localized and current on the one hand, and, on the other, one that will largely stand the test of time. Indeed, whether you are a buyer or a seller or even an agent, and no matter what market you're in—i.e. a seller's market, a buyer's market, or even in a balanced market—so much of the information provided in this book is universal and pertains to all. All sellers share the common goal of presenting their properties in the best light, as is detailed in Chapters 5 and 8. Likewise, if you are a buyer, no matter your market you will need to be well-versed on such topics as financing, credit, disclosures, and the like, which we have outlined throughout the book and in detail in Chapter 7. And everyone—whether buyer, seller, or agent—can benefit from our tried-and-true advice on conventional real estate etiquette and protocol; even in real estate one must always be mindful of one's manners and keep the focus on building a productive partnership, thereby fostering a smooth transaction. In short, this book—though area-specific—was designed to provide comprehensive, life-long guidance, of the sort that can be heeded in this generation and the next.

We hope you have benefited, and will continue to benefit from, the resources and insights we have compiled for you in our East Bay *Insider's Guide*. Now that you are familiar with our real estate philosophies and methods (The Art of Real Estate – Educate, Communicate, Inspire), it is our greatest hope that you will feel both comfortable and confident coming to us with any and all of your real estate needs, questions, concerns, and goals. As the publication of this book makes clear, we pride ourselves on our transparency and earnest desire to communicate with you – please do not hesitate to reach out to us now or in the future.

All our best wishes!

Debbi DiMaggio & Adam Betta

APPENDICES

APPENDIX A:

Advice from Bay Area Photographer-Director
Quentin C. Bacon
Blogging to Find Your Voice

Since 2010, Debbi DiMaggio and photographer-director Quentin Bacon have shared a dynamic and mutually beneficial partnership. Quentin, a San Francisco-based professional photographer specializing in editorial, advertising and portrait photography, is Debbi's go-to artist when it comes to capturing moments that matter. Whether it's before-and-after shots of a listed property, professional headshots, or personal keepsakes, all of Quentin's stunning photographs tell a unique story. And that is exactly what Quentin has helped Debbi to do as well: to tell her own story.

To Quentin, the real estate world involves wearing many hats. It encompasses scheduling, financing, photography, remodeling, networking, negotiating, construction, interfacing, and many other factors. From working with Realtors® like Debbi, Quentin has come to appreciate the unique depth of knowledge and the diversity of skill sets that Realtors® possess. He finds that most real estate agents don't realize how interesting and unique their insights are, and how much consumers might benefit from them. To bridge this gap between agent and consumer, Quentin encouraged Debbi to begin maintaining a blog. A blog, he told her, would showcase her individual voice so that clients and potential clients could get to know Debbi specifically. Now, thanks to Quentin's encouragement and guidance—as well as the numerous striking photographs that adorn each and every post—Debbi writes and manages multiple blogs and websites, including:

- ❖ www.DebbiDiMaggioBlog.com – A Grateful Life
- ❖ www.DebbiDiMaggioLifestyle.com
- ❖ www.DiMaggioAndBetta.com

Quentin emphasizes the positive benefits blogging can have for the author, as well as the readers. Blogging forces Debbi to do her real estate homework, in a sense – it forces her to reflect on what she's done and what she's learned, and then to articulate this clearly and compellingly, in such a way that her clientele will understand and be engaged. Because she has already articulated her professional thoughts on her blog, Debbi then is even more prepared to speak with clients in person; she knows how to craft each experience into a well-written story. Blogging also gives Realtors® a platform from which to defend the properties they have listed. Undoubtedly, houses may attract negative comments from online viewers or from those who don't understand the property's potential like a Realtor® would. With a blog, an agent can make a constructive counterargument and provide buyers with the concrete facts about a property—rather than allowing them to believe negative gossip.

Along with these many benefits, Quentin acknowledges that blogging comes with its consequences: once Debbi's unique, personal voice has been exposed to the public, it is bound to resonate with some and to offend others. In this sense, some risk and vulnerability is involved in blogging – a Realtor®'s blog might fend off clients as well as attract them. But, as Quentin and Debbi both know, blogging is worth the risk. As a real estate agent, you want to find clients who want to work with you for who you truly are. Those readers who connect with Debbi's writing style and individual voice are the ones who will make a good fit as clients.

Many Realtors® are indifferent to social media and believe they are too busy to put in the time required to maintain a strong online presence. These agents may also feel that time spent blogging or connecting online is wasted, since it may not contribute directly to a boost to their incomes. While it's more than likely that social media accounts do help professionals to bring in clients, this is not the final purpose—whether blogging and social media accounts help one's income or not, at least they help agents to communicate. An agent with a blog is more than just a commodity. When you have a means of connecting to your clients you become more than just any old photographer or Realtor®—you are one with a voice.

See a sampling of Debbi's blog posts (and other featured articles) in Appendix B, below.

In addition, Debbi's social media accounts—on sites such as Twitter, Facebook, Foursquare, Pinterest, and Houzz—all thrive. For Debbi, each of these blogs and websites provides a platform from which to live out her real estate mantra: Educate, Communicate, and Inspire. To connect with Debbi, follow her at these links:

* Facebook: www.Facebook.com/Debbi.DiMaggio
* Instagram: www.Instagram.com/DebbiDiMaggio
* Twitter: www.Twitter.com/DebbiDiMaggio
* LinkedIn: www.LinkedIn.com/in/DebbiDiMaggio14
* Pinterest: www.Pinterest.com/DebbiDiMaggio/
* YouTube: www.YouTube.com/user/DebbiDiMaggio
* Houzz: www.Houzz.com/pro/DebbiDiMaggio
* Foursquare: www.Foursquare.com/DebbiDiMaggio

APPENDIX B:
Debbi's Blog Posts & Feature Articles

"Preparing Your Home for Market"
Piedmont Patch, Patch.com
by Debbi DiMaggio

One of my favorite aspects of real estate is project management and using my creative skills to bring a home from "lived in" to "staged to sell"

A Convenient Checklist

Real estate has many aspects. One of my favorites is when a seller surrenders their home to me and my team so we can take their home from "lived in" to "staged to sell." As a professional Realtor®, it is one of the services I provide. However, if you wish to do it yourself, here is a brief recap of what I recommend.

A Note to Friends: When I walk into a home with my "Realtor® Hat" on, I look at the home in a completely different way than if I was invited into a home for a social occasion.

Planning: I begin with a walk through, assessing the property and home with a keen eye. What I scrutinize: curb appeal, gardens, walkways, light fixtures, paint, floors, carpet, appliances, hardware, rooms and bathrooms, fireplace, electrical, furnace, the basement and, finally, the foundation. I inquire about systems you cannot easily see like the roof and the sewer. I take it all in, commit to memory, and visualize a plan. Window washing, a detailed cleaning and staging are the finishing touches after we complete the mini, or not so mini, makeover.

Preparation: Whether we are working on the transformation together, or should you decide to do it on your own, obtaining bids is the next step. I have a team of amazing service providers who will meet with me at a moment's notice, so I am able to line up everyone over a one or two-day period in order to obtain our estimates. Upon receiving the bids, I then sit down with the sellers and review ... how much we will do, what makes financial sense, and highlight what is mandatory. Then we prioritize, together. Preparing a home for market, depending on the amount of work to be done, on average can take between 10 days and three weeks. This also allows time to for me to create the advertising and online presence before the home goes to market.

Transformation: A commitment from the homeowner and attention to detail is critical as there is much work involved. Typically this entails removing clutter, exchanging old furniture for new, and adding beautiful accessories. There are many talented stagers and designers who are wonderful to work with during this process. I've also been known to make a dozen trips to various supply stores to find just the right appliances, fixtures or hardware for a client. By partnering with my wonderful resource providers, we can create a flawless transition. From "lived in" to "staged to sell", the transformation is exciting each and every time.

The risk: Clients love their home so much, that sometimes they want to stay!

"Preparing a Masterpiece // My Newest Listing: Sea View Avenue, Piedmont"

DebbiDiMaggioBlog.com
by Debbi DiMaggio

Preparing a home for market…

A blank canvas—I walk the entire home up and down, in and around, to get a feel for it. Then I discuss what it may need and get an idea of what the homeowner is willing to do and not do. This particular home does not have young children so there are no plastic toys and excess clothes of all ages filling the closets, hallways, playrooms and attic. And the furniture is all very expensive and in good condition – however, with that said we have to take into consideration that the home will be looked at by people, young and mature, with varied tastes and styles. So, after I have a feeling for the space and the home, I bring in my first team: Kelly Banks of Designing Women Interiors, MB Jesse, Painting Contractors, and the homeowners' daughter, Kimberly, who happens to be my longtime friend. We all collaborate and share ideas. We all have a varied perspective. My inner voices come from those of homebuyers—I hear what they will say. I'm not a "homebuyer whisperer," but my intuition and gut always put me on top. Now, Kim, an artist with a keen sense of design, sees a different angle while Kelly helps bring it back to "staging," not "living". Be sure there were 3 opinions, just like today when we hung art. I just have to brag a little. Michelle, our Art Consultant, and Kim, an Artist herself, were leaning towards a darker, less contrasting piece while I loved the piece that ended up hanging on the wall. The Art that we hung had strokes of green and blue that pulled in the green plants and blue water from the view. The other piece was, yes, a great masterpiece, but, like others, I would be drawn to analyzing the

ART and not enjoying the room and the view. I won I won! A Realtor®'s point of view is one that knows and anticipates the homebuyers' thoughts and objections—and with that we try to mitigate what we can. I love that too! The PROCESS, each and every step of the way.

"The Importance of Staging // Before & After"
DebbiDiMaggioBlog.com
by Debbi DiMaggio

Buyers begin their search online.

Due to the Internet and social media sites like Facebook and Pinterest, it is imperative that Realtors® impress upon their Sellers the importance of staging their home prior to market. Beautiful homes, lovely interior details, and quality furnishings are necessary in order to entice a Buyer to preview a home in person. Staging has become common practice, and Buyers will either rule out a home or choose to preview that home in person, should the photographs they see online capture their interest. If they do not like what they see, they may not take the time to visit the home in person, thus losing a potential Buyer and sale.

One of the most important parts of a Realtor®'s job is guiding their clients for success. It's all in the preparation. Once a home hits the market, the waiting begins.

"Home Maintenance Checklist // Does your home need a checkup?"
DebbiDiMaggioBlog.com
by Debbi DiMaggio

As we enter into the fall and winter seasons, you may want to take care of

a few things around your home. Here is a Home Maintenance Checklist to consider.

One of the most common issues that arise as we are getting our properties ready for market is that the Sewer Lateral is broken, off-set, or cracked. This is something that will eventually need to be addressed when you sell your home but, more importantly, if cracks are evident you will want to replace the Sewer Lateral for the well-being of your family. Learn more on the EBMUD website.

Do you have a CO Detector on each level of your home?

This is now a Point of Sale Ordinance and is something you will want to install in your home for safety. In that same vein, please test or replace your Smoke Detector batteries. Many times we say to ourselves – it won't happen to us, why bother, or I will do it tomorrow.

Our daughter Bianca is attending college at CU Boulder and has just experienced one of the worst floods on record, as per the media. When we were going through orientation—the students had their orientation and, yes, parents had an orientation of their own—4 days long! I admit I cut a session one afternoon; I was overwhelmed with information and had been taking lots and lots of notes! (As is my nature). I then proceeded, like all parents, to reiterate everything I learned back to Bianca who said, "MOM I know!" I remember quite vividly, however, the presenter telling us to make sure our students signed up for the text ALERT System. At the time I was wary and a bit nervous, thinking why would they need an ALERT? What could go wrong? I recall feeling, on the one hand, relieved that they were on top of things, but on the flip-side was anxious that some huge disaster could happen while our daughter Bianca was so far away from us!

During the past week Bianca has been sent multiple text message alerts keeping the residents informed of Flash Floods and other important messages including evacuation notices. All that to say, take warnings seriously, even if you think it won't happen to you.

Which reminds me — Do you have your Earthquake Disaster Kit on hand?

Please do not be overwhelmed by the list. Implement the Slight Edge Principle:

"The principal method of the Slight Edge is doing seemingly small, insignificant steps consistently in the right direction. Over time all the seemingly small steps add up to massive action toward the ultimate success in what you seek." Of course, this principle can be used in all aspects of your life; including goal setting, studies, exercise, diet, and in your job.

Let's Get Started!

Monthly Home Maintenance Checklist
- Fire Extinguisher: Check that it's fully charged; recharge or replace if needed.
- Sink/Tub Stoppers and Drain Holes: Clean out debris.
- Garbage Disposal: Flush with hot water and baking soda. Do the same for your Dishwasher.
- Forced-Air Heating System: Change filters once a month if user's manual recommends fiberglass filters.

- Range Hood: Clean grease filter.
- Floor and Outdoor Drain Grates: Clean out debris.

Twice a Year

- Smoke Detector: Test batteries and replace if needed.
- Toilet: Check for leaks and water run-on.
- Interior Caulking: Inspect caulking around tubs, showers, and sinks; replace any if it is deteriorating.
- Forced-Air Heating System: Change semi-annually if user's manual recommends high efficiency pleated or HEPA-style filters. You can find at Ace Hardware or Home Depot.
- Garbage Disposal: Tighten drain connections and fasteners.
- Clothes Washer: Clean water inlet filters; check hoses and replace them if they are leaking.
- Clothes Dryer: Vacuum lint from ducts and surrounding areas.
- Wiring: Check for frayed cords and wires; repair or replace them as needed. Do you still have a FUSE Box? Consider upgrading your electrical system. This is a valuable upgrade to perform ahead of time, prior to selling your home one day. Do you have a FEDERAL PACIFIC Panel? If so, consider replacement.
- Range Hood: Wash fan blades and housing.

Spring Cleaning

- Roof: Inspect roof surface, flashing, eaves, and soffits; repair if needed. Please ask for a referral. Inspecting the roof is one of the inspections we highly recommend prior to market. Don't wait until you go to sell your home; have it looked at sooner to avoid compounded expenses from deferred maintenance.
- Gutters and Downspouts: Clean them out or install no-clean version. Inspect and repair weak areas; check for proper drainage and make repairs if needed.
- Siding: Inspect and clean siding and repair if needed.
- Exterior Caulking: Inspect caulking and replace any that is deteriorating.

- Windowsills, Doorsills, and Thresholds: Fill cracks, caulk edges, repaint; replace if needed. Due to the harshness of sun and varied weather conditions your windowsills, doorsills and thresholds should be monitored and cared for whether painted or wood-stained. Don't wait another 7-10 years before you repaint to refresh or renew your sills. Put this one on your rotation list every 1-3 years, as necessary.
- Window and Door Screens: Clean screening and repair or replace if needed; tighten or repair any loose or damaged frames and repaint if needed; replace broken, worn, or missing hardware; tighten and lubricate door hinges and closers.

When we sell a home, we prefer to have all screens removed for a cleaner look. Area standards vary from county to county, city to city, but most agents would counsel you to remove the screens and store in the garage as well.

Windows Washed, Inside and Out: Hire a professional to clean the interior and exterior of your windows. It isn't a huge investment, so don't wait until you sell your home to enjoy this fresh look.

Summer is Over – Fall Checklist
- Roof: Inspect roof surface, flashing, eaves, and soffits; repair if needed. If you delay on this item you may find yourself making an emergency call during heavy rains or worse, during the holidays.
- Gutters and Downspouts: Clean out. Inspect and repair weak points; check for proper slope. Be sure the downspouts are not pointing towards the foundation but are directed away from the foundation so as not to compromise the structure and/or cause water damage.
- Chimney or Stovepipe: Clean flue (more frequently if needed); repair any cracks in flue or any loose or crumbling mortar. Earthquake Retrofit: Check to see if the chimney is braced and secured as necessary. Also make sure a damper is present. Oftentimes, in older

homes, the damper is not operable and the chimney has not been used or inspected for many years.

- Siding: Inspect and clean siding and repair if needed.
- Exterior Caulking: Inspect caulking and replace any that is deteriorating.
- Windows and Doors: Replace any cracked or broken glass; tighten or repair any loose or damaged frames and repaint if needed. Replace damaged hardware; tighten and lubricate door hinges and closers.
- Window and Door Weather Stripping: Inspect and repair or replace if it is deteriorating or if it does not seal.
- Thermostat: Clean heat sensor, contact points, and contacts; check accuracy and replace thermostat if it is not functioning properly.
- Outdoor Faucets: Calling All You Lake Tahoe Homeowners—If you live in an area with freezing winters, be sure to maintain your shut off valves to outdoor faucets. Open spigots and drain, store hoses. Also be sure to contact your local Realtor® to obtain a Checklist for Cold Weather Homeowners. The same goes for those snowbirds who head to Scottsdale, Florida, or other warm weather areas – There are a host of items one needs to be aware of when you live in those climates as well. We built and owned a home in Scottsdale for many years—so watch out for those scorpions and be sure to install a water softener, to name a few.

Once Per Year
- Main Cleanout Drain: Have a "rooter" professional clean out the main line, particularly if there are mature trees in your yard whose roots could have cracked the pipe in their search for moisture.
- HVAC System: Have a professional tune up your heat/air conditioning system.

Other Important Action Items

- Water Heater Safety: Is your water heater braced and strapped to today's standards? Do you have a pressure relief valve? Does the pipe terminate outside of the home or away from a living space? If not, you should add this to the top of your list.
- Painting: Every 7-10 years it is a good idea to repaint the exterior. We paint all our homes a variation of a gray-green color by Benjamin Moore. I love the way it blends with the gardens and the light.
- Termite Inspection: It is a good idea to have a termite inspection to find out what has occurred over the years and what you might address long before you go to sell your home.
- Driveway: Repair and seal driveway.
- Exterior Decks: Pressure wash decks. Check and apply sealer to decks.
- Garden: Fertilize the lawn. Keep up your garden in the front and back. If you let it go it will be quite costly to bring it back to life.
- Trees: Trim trees and shrubs touching your home. Keep limbs off of wires. Hiring an arborist to trim oversized trees before they get out of hand is desirable. This can be a costly expense if you wait too long.

Set the Stage

Don't wait to make your home picture perfect,

    and…

    Remember to take it one step at a time.

    But do address the checklist for the health and safety of your home, your family and your pocketbook.

If you would like a service provider referral please contact either Adam or myself; we have cultivated many resources and relationships over the years. If you are interested in having us assess repairs or prepare your home for market we welcome your call. Adam and I have been guiding and counseling clients for over 20 years and we look forward to helping you too.

Thank you for taking the time to read my
blog, DebbiDiMaggioAGratefulLife.com

Fondly,

Debbi DiMaggio
The Art of Real Estate // Educate, Communicate, Inspire

"Sound Off"
SFGate.com, SF Gate Real Estate
featuring Debbi DiMaggio

Q: How much does having a swimming pool add to a property in the Oakland, Piedmont and Berkeley area?

A: It doesn't add much value here, and many buyers see a pool as a negative, some going as far as filling in the pool as soon as they buy it.

In fact, one of my favorite homes in Piedmont as a child was recently sold, and the pool was filled because they had young children and thought it was too much of a risk.

My new home does have a pool, and as a mother of two teenagers, I know my kids and their friends will be spending a lot of time at our home, and I love that. But the weather isn't always conducive to having a pool, and a lot of buyers here will not consider offering on a home that has one.

- Debbi DiMaggio

"Piedmont: West Coast Mayberry with great schools"
SFGate.com
by Valerie Fahey
featuring Debbi DiMaggio

If the city of Piedmont—approximately 11,000 people in 1.7 square miles of land—conjures up anything, it is probably green streets and greenbacks.

By the 1920s, Piedmont was known as the city of millionaires because it had the most per square mile of any U.S. city. Time seems to have only enhanced that colorful reputation, now complemented by tree-lined streets, green parks and even median strips planted with flowers.

Known today for its top-notch public schools, this well-heeled city survived annexation efforts in the early 1900s and today thrives with a great quality of life and as a place to raise a family.

Recent figures show that 71 percent of the city's 3,804 households consist of married couples and 47 percent have children younger than 18.

Piedmont is surrounded by the city of Oakland. While Piedmont provides its own fire department, police and schools, it shares other services; Oakland meets the needs for a public library and post office, plus most retail services.

A small commercial district in the center of town includes three banks (Wells Fargo, Citibank and Bank of America), a real estate office, Mulberry's Market, a gas station and a few professional offices. The city is served by two weekly newspapers: the Piedmonter, a neighborhood newspaper owned by the Contra Costa Times, and the citizen-run Piedmont Post.

The town has all the charm of a West Coast "Mayberry R.F.D.," reflecting the 1960s TV show of Andy Griffith fame. And it's also unfailingly eco-friendly. Piedmont has received the National Arbor Day Foundation's Tree City USA designation for several years running. "It has 44 acres of parkland and 25 different varieties of trees," said Park and Projects Manager Mark Feldkamp.

Why residents love it

Six years ago, Laura Pochop was living in San Francisco with her husband, Chad Olcott.

"We loved the Mission," Pochop said. "But with a child about to enter kindergarten, we were looking for a community where we could send our kids all the way through high school in the public school system."

It was Thanksgiving weekend when they came to view an open house. "We fell in love. It was so tranquil and walkable with stunning views," she said.

The one thing they didn't find were family-run stores like those dotting the Mission District, where you could walk and get a good cup of joe or buy an ice cream cone for the kids. So not only did they buy a house, but two years ago, Olcott and Pochop opened Mulberry's, where they now serve Peet's coffee, Fentons ice cream and all the grocery basics.

Mayberry-esque gatherings are the backbone of small towns, and Piedmont has a plethora of school fundraisers, a kitschy Fourth of July Parade, an annual holiday tree-lighting ceremony and the Piedmont Turkey Trot, a 3-mile fun run benefiting the school track and cross-country teams on Thanksgiving.

Because of its school system, low crime rate, good weather, short commute to San Francisco and high property values, it is regarded as one of the most desirable residential communities in the Bay Area. Piedmont was ranked No. 21 of the 25 top-earning towns in CNN-Money Magazine's list of "The Best Places to Live in 2007," and was also named the

"Best Place to Live" in the United States in 2007 by Forbes. The public high school was ranked in the top 500 in the nation by Newsweek.

"What attracts families to Piedmont are both the fine schools and its small-town feel," said Teresa Baum of Pacific Union Realty. "Housing prices have been among the most stable in the region, even during the downturn."

Since January, there have been 65 sales of single-family homes, listed from $750,000 to $6.5 million. **Debbi DiMaggio**, an agent who has lived in Piedmont for 45 years, said, "It's close to everything. San Francisco is just 30 minutes away, and you can be through the tunnel into Contra Costa in half that time."

Piedmont's origins

The biggest issues in Piedmont usually revolve around the schools and land use. One debate is whether the new sports field surface at Havens Elementary should be grass, crumb rubber infill or turf with coconut husk and cork infill. A more contentious sports field question is playing out along busy Moraga Road, a.k.a. Blair Park, where proponents want two soccer fields and neighbors don't.

The area that is now the city of Piedmont was once part of a 14,330-acre land grant, given by the king of Spain in 1820 to Presidio soldier Don Luis Peralta. The region's early history is dominated by Peralta's ranch lands and the efforts of missionaries.

During the late Victorian era, other men were drawn to the area. The president of Western Union, James Gamble, bought 350 acres of land from Walter Blair, built a mansion for himself, and intended to build homes on the remainder of his property. He christened the enterprise the Piedmont Land Co., and this is the origin of the name that would eventually be given to the city.

The importance of schools also can be traced to the town's origins.

In 1905, residents of the then-unincorporated area outside Oakland passed a bond to build a school on Piedmont Avenue. When the city of Oakland took over the school and had the audacity to send tax bills to residents who had supported the bond, Piedmont started plotting to become a city of its own.

Notable residents

In January 1907, Piedmonters voted to incorporate, and on Jan. 31, they became residents of the state's newest city.

Many professional athletes call Piedmont home, including ex-National Football League stars Bubba Paris and Bill Romanowski and ex-Major League Baseball player Dave McCarty. There's also newly appointed ambassador to Australia Jeff Bleich, and Peter Docter, director of Pixar movies including "Monsters, Inc." and "Up."
Don't forget to say hello to Green Day lead singer Billie Joe Armstrong or drummer Tre Cool when you see them out walking down the town's well-manicured streets.

Piedmont

Population: 10,952

White: 78.59 percent

Asian: 16.02 percent

Two or more races: 3.38 percent

African American: 1.24 percent

Housing units: 3,859

Per-capita income: $70,539

Median home value: $1,073,700

Median resident age: 43.7

"An Enchanted Life // Home, Family, Heart"
DebbiDiMaggioBlog.com
by Debbi DiMaggio

Every time I have the good fortune to work on a new listing I am excited for the opportunity. For some reason I never get tired or bored with the process. Today while having lunch in San Francisco at the St. Francis Yacht Club someone asked if I had separate blogs (a real estate blog and a personal blog). I explained how my entire life overlaps. For one, Real Estate does not feel like a job to me, it never has. It is just another aspect of my day. It is just a part of me. I love to educate, share and inspire. Whether I am reminding my audience to book their annual doctor appointments through a story, find a workout routine that makes them happy, share a new restaurant, a personal story, happy or sad, detail something I learned and hope that my story might help another, promote an event you may want to attend or a charity you might want to join, a great app or some fabulous find, a vacation destination, a family story, or simply to share a beautiful and interesting home or opportunity.

Debbi DiMaggio Blog, aka Debbi DiMaggio a Grateful Life, encompasses all of the things I love and enjoy each and every day. I hope you enjoy my blog and that my blog inspires you to create your own bundle of happiness in life.

Debbi DiMaggio
Realtor®, Marketing and Social Marketing Guru
Philanthropist, Community Ambassador and Mentor
Contact Me: debbi@debbidimaggio.com
Real Estate Website: www.DiMaggioAndBetta.com
Read my Blog: www.DebbiDiMaggioAGratefulLife.com
Giving Back: www.DebbiDiMaggioLifestyle.com

"Impeccable Marketing Generates Listings"
Monday Morning Radio Show
featuring Debbi DiMaggio

Using exceptional, professional and consistent marketing materials for all of your listings is a sure way to generate new listings. It doesn't matter if you're marketing a $300,000 house or a million dollar-plus house, all listings should use the same professional marketing materials. This was the heart of Debbi DiMaggio's message recently when she was featured on a recent Monday Morning Radio Show, "How to Generate Listings Using Your Property Marketing."

"Market every property the same regardless of its list price. You do this because your next seller may hire you based on the marketing they saw on another one of your properties. People are watching the quality of who you are and what you produce," said Debbi. She added that her signature marketing is one of the key elements of the value proposition she presents to clients.

During the interview with company COO Keith Robinson, Debbi outlined some of her basic marketing strategies and favorite tools:

- Every listing has its own website and includes a virtual tour provided by TourFactory.
- Every listing is professionally photographed and the images are used on the range of marketing materials from flyers, postcards, brochures and websites to local news media print marketing materials. There are many benefits to amassing a database of professional images of her listings—from maintaining property libraries on the range of websites to using the images in listing presentations for

similar properties. In this internet age, agents' listing images are visible worldwide and featuring only professional images will do wonders to help an agent build an impeccable brand.

- Debbi also uses print marketing including Just Listed and Just Sold postcards, quarterly market reports customized for a particular farm, image-rich and colorful flyers—and not MLS sheets—in sign boxes and local newsprint ads; all of which contain the quality, professional images featured online.

"Many agents put a lot of work into obtaining a listing and then skimp on marketing because a property's price is the key factor that will determine how quickly it will sell. To use this strategy alone is tantamount to quitting at the finish line and wastes a valuable opportunity to receive additional listings. Agents who go the extra mile and use all of the professional marketing tools available, including professional photographers and stagers, will reap a greater benefit from their efforts," said Debbi.

If you missed Debbi's presentation, be sure to listen now. She also covered the details of enhanced listings and how to boost a property's internet presence on real estate sites and social media.

Copy and paste **https://www.youtube.com/watch?v=DhOEBhug2hA** into your browser to listen to the show and view slides of Debbi's marketing materials.

APPENDIX C:

Sample Buyer's Net Sheet

Breakdown of a buyer's net payment, for a theoretical property in Piedmont, CA, with a purchase price of $1,500,000. Includes buyer's fraction of the city transfer tax (50%), and assumes a down payment of 20% of the purchase price.

First American Title Company
6232 La Salle Avenue
Oakland, CA 94611

Estimated Settlement Statement

Property: TBD; Piedmont, CA
Buyer(s): DiMaggio/Betta
Seller(s): As Vested

File No: TBD
Officer: Renee Haugen
Loan No: TBD
Settlement Date: TBD

Buyer Charge	Buyer Credit	Charge Description	Seller Charge	Seller Credit
$1,500,000.00		Purchase Price		
		Commission (Paid by seller)		
	$1,200,000.00	New Loan		
$1,870.00		Escrow Fee		
$2,979.00		Owners Title Policy		
$1,016.00		Lenders Title Policy		
$125.00		Notary (IF APPLICABLE)		
$200.00		Recording Fees		
		County Transfer Tax (Paid by seller)		
$9,750.00		City Transfer Tax (1/2)		
$2,800.00		Homeowners Insurance		
		Pro-Rated Property Taxes (Estimated)		
		Natural Hazard Report		
		Plus Lender's Fees as disclosed		
	$318,740.00	Cash From Borrower	Cash From/To Seller	
$1,518,740.00	$1,518,740.00	Totals	$0.00	$0.00

First American Title Company
6232 La Salle Avenue Oakland, CA 94611
Estimated Settlement Statement

Property: Piedmont, CA
Officer: Renee Haugen
Buyer(s): Debbi DiMaggio abs Adam Betta
Loan No: TBD
Seller(s): As Vested
Settlement Date: TBD
Purchase Price: $1,500,000.00
Commission: Paid by seller
New Loan: $1,200,000.00
Escrow Fee: $1,870.00
Owners Title Policy: $2,979.00
Lenders Title Policy: $1,016.00
Notary (IF APPLICABLE): $125.00
Recording Fees: $200.00
County Transfer Tax: Paid by seller
City Transfer Tax (1/2): $9,750.00
Homeowners Insurance: $2,800.00
Pro-Rated Property Taxes (Estimated)
Natural Hazard Report
TC/Online Access/ etc (If applicable): $500.00
Plus Lender's Fees as disclosed

Cash From Borrower: $318,740.00
Totals: $1,518,740.00

** Both city and county transfer taxes differ from location to location; this is solely an example. Please contact your Realtor® for accurate estimates specifically related to your home purchase.

APPENDIX D:

Sample Seller's Net Sheet

Breakdown of a seller's net proceeds, for a theoretical property in Oakland, CA, with a selling price of $1,500,000.

First American Title Company
6232 La Salle Avenue
Oakland, CA 94611

Estimated Settlement Statement

Property:	Oakland, CA		File No:	
			Officer:	Renee Haugen
Buyer(s):	TBD		Loan No:	TBD
Seller(s):	As Vested		Settlement Date:	TBD

Buyer Charge	Buyer Credit	Charge Description	Seller Charge	Seller Credit
		Purchase Price		$1,500,000.00
		Commission	$90,000.00	
		New Loan		
		Escrow Fee		
		Owners Title Policy		
		Lenders Title Policy		
		Notary (IF APPLICABLE)	$125.00	
		Recording Fees	$100.00	
		County Transfer Tax	$1,650.00	
		City Transfer Tax (1/2)	$11,250.00	
		Homeowners Insurance		
		Pro-Rated Property Taxes (Estimated)	$2,718.00	
		Natural Hazard Report	$125.00	
		TC/Online Access/ etc (If applicable)	$500.00	
		Payoff if applicable - per lender		
		Cash From/To Borrower	Cash To Seller	$1,393,532.00	
$0.00	$0.00	Totals	$1,500,000.00	$1,500,000.00

First American Title Company
6232 La Salle Avenue Oakland, CA 94611
Estimated Settlement Statement

Property: Oakland, CA
Officer: Renee Haugen
Buyer(s): TBD
Loan No: TBD
Seller(s): As Vested
Settlement Date: TBD
Purchase Price: $1,500,000.00
Commission: $90,000.00
New Loan
Notary (IF APPLICABLE): $125.00
Recording Fees: $100.00
County Transfer Tax: $1,650.00
City Transfer Tax (1/2): $11,250.00
Homeowners Insurance:
Pro-Rated Property Taxes (Estimated): $2,718.00
Natural Hazard Report: $125.00
TC/Online Access/ etc (If applicable): $500.00
Payoff if applicable - per lender

Cash to Seller: $1,393,532.00
Totals: $1,500,000.00

GLOSSARY OF TERMS

*All terms found in this glossary appear in **bold font** at the first instance that they appear in the body of the text.*

Agent: A real estate agent is anyone who has earned a real estate license and is therefore qualified to assist clients in the purchase and sale of property. Requirements vary by state, but all agents must take a certain number of courses and pass an exam to earn their real estate license.

Appraisal: An estimation in writing of the price of a property, which draws on the sale prices of other, comparable sold homes in the area. The appraisal is carried out by the bank providing the buyer's loan, and represents an accurate estimate of a home's value.

Appraiser: The individual who carries out an appraisal and is trained to evaluate and judge the value of a given property. Appraisers might work independently or for a mortgage lender. Banks can refer reliable local appraisers.

Area Standards: Also known as "as is" customary, area standards refer to the various practices that are conventional in a given market. Each real estate market has its own customs and conventions to follow.

Asking Price (a.k.a. Listing Price): In real estate, the asking price is the amount at which a property is offered for sale. The asking price is determined by the home seller, ideally with the help of an agent's suggestions and a comparative market analysis (CMA). The price at which the home actually sells is determined by buyers and the state of the current market.

Bidding War: A circumstance that arises when multiple buyers are interested in the same property and consequently attempt to outbid each other to become the new owners, driving the home's price increasingly higher. Bidding wars are common in seller's markets and typically move at a very fast pace.

Broker: A real estate broker is a person who has qualified to earn a real estate license and has received additional education to pass a broker's license exam. A broker is licensed to own, manage, or operate their own brokerage, and seeks to connect sellers to interested buyers. Brokers can work on their own or can hire agents to work under them.

Broker Tour: An open house held for real estate agents, during the week day. In our market, the broker tour (or agent tour) is typically held on a Monday or Thursday depending on where the home is located.

Buyer's Agent (a.k.a. Selling Agent): A real estate agent who represents the buyer in a given transaction, helping him or her to locate a property to purchase.

"Buyer's Market": When home inventory is high and supply exceeds demand, the resulting situation is called a "buyer's market." This is because buyers have the advantage over homeowners in price negotiations. Also referred to as a "cold market."

City Transfer Tax: A tax collected by a city whenever property exchanges hands or is sold in the public records. These taxes vary from city to city and are customarily split equally between the buyer and the seller. At $13.00 per $1,000 and $15.00 per $1,000 respectively, the city transfer taxes for Piedmont and Oakland are some of the highest. Also known as real property conveyance tax.

Close of Escrow (COE): Refers to the transfer of title. Also known as the closing or the settlement. A transaction is typically considered "closed" once all documents have been signed, the money has changed hands, and the sale has been verified and recorded at the local recorder's office. The close of escrow time period refers to the length of time allotted to close the deal (usually 14-21 days in a competitive market, though 30 days on average).

Closing Costs: Any expenses incurred by buyers or sellers in the completion of a real estate transaction, apart from the price of the property itself. These might include loan origination fees, appraisal fees, title insurance, taxes, and surveys. Closing costs are divided up into nonrecurring costs and prepaid costs; the former refers to one-time costs associated with the new mortgage, while the latter refers to those costs that will recur over time (such as homeowners' insurance and property taxes).

Commission: The monetary fee paid to an agent or other professional as compensation for the work they do. In our local markets, commission is about 6% of the sale price of the home, and is split equally between the buyer's and the seller's agent (i.e. 3% each). It is customary that the seller always pays both agents' commissions out of the proceeds from the sale.

Comparable Sales (a.k.a. "Comps"): Also known as comparables or comparable properties, "comps" are other properties similar to the property being appraised. "Comps" must be homes of similar size and attributes that have recently sold in the same area. Agents and appraisers utilize "comps" as a means of estimating a home's fair market value.

Comparative Market Analysis (CMA): A comparative study of similar properties that recently sold in a given area. Real estate agents provide buyers and sellers with CMAs to help them determine offer prices and list prices, respectively. A CMA is similar to, but less formal than, a professional appraisal.

Contingency: A condition that must be met before a contract becomes legally binding. For instance, a buyer may say their offer to purchase a home is contingent upon the home achieving a satisfactory home inspection report. The most common contingencies in our area are home or property inspection contingencies and appraisal and loan contingencies. In other areas, offers are sometimes made that are contingent upon the buyers' ability to first sell their current home; this is rarely ever seen in our market. Offers to purchase a home are most competitive when no contingencies are specified, and the offer is therefore non-contingent.

Counteroffer: When a buyer makes an offer to purchase a house, the seller can present a counteroffer in response, suggesting amendments to the original offer that make it more appealing to the seller. Counteroffers can be made verbally or in writing, and can go back and forth between seller and buyer multiple times before an acceptable compromise is reached. In competitive markets like ours, buyers are happy to receive counteroffers since this gives them a second chance.

County Transfer Tax: A tax collected by a county whenever real property exchanges hands or is sold in the public records. The seller pays 100% of the county transfer tax as is customary in our local markets of Berkeley, Oakland, and Piedmont (though this custom varies from market to market).

Credit Report: An official record of a person's current and past debt repayment history. Lenders utilize credit reports to determine whether or not a borrower makes debt payments on time and is therefore a strong candidate for a loan. The three major credit agencies that maintain and sell copies of one's credit report are: Experian, Equifax, and TransUnion.

Credit Score: A number used to evaluate one's credit history, taken from the information supplied in the credit report. A credit score is useful to lenders because it presents a quick and objective summary of an individual's credit history. Lower credit scores are associated with more risk for the lender, while higher credit scores make a lender feel confident that the person will make payments on time.

"Curb Appeal": This term refers to the initial attractiveness and appeal of a property as it is seen from the exterior, or from the curb. Seller's agents often tell sellers to increase their property's curb appeal by investing in a new paint job, landscaping, and window washing. Strong curb appeal helps add value to a property and attracts buyers to open houses.

Disclosure: The act of divulging all the relevant information related to a property that may influence an investment decision. When sellers decide to place their home on the market, their agents encourage them to disclose every possible detail about their home's renovation and repair history, so that buyers can be fully confident and knowledgeable regarding the state of the property. It is always best to err on the side of over-disclosure, since unhappy buyers could potentially pursue legal action if something significant was left undisclosed.

Real estate agents are legally bound to disclose anything they know that could affect the value of a property.

Disclosure Packet: A portfolio of information related to the history and condition of a home being sold. The disclosure packet is the history of a property provided by the seller to potential buyers and their agents so that they are familiar with the quality of a home they are interested in purchasing. A typical disclosure packet from our area will contain the following: multiple regional and state disclosures, questionnaires, a list of improvements made over the years along with supporting documentation, a home or general inspection report and any other reports (such as roof, sewer lateral, or termite), a natural hazards disclosure, a preliminary title report, a permit history and a sidewalk inspection. The contents of disclosure packets differ depending on the customs of a particular city.

Down Payment: A payment which reflects a percentage of the purchase price of the home a buyer is placing in contract. Typically the percentage is 20% of the purchase price, but sometimes it can be as low as 10-15%, or oftentimes it can be as high as 30-50% down. It all depends on the buyer's financial situation. A bank/lender wants to know that the buyer has "skin in the game" – thus their requirement that there be a down payment in order to obtain a loan from the lender.

Dual Agency: A "disclosed dual agent" represents the interests of both the seller and the buyer during the same transaction. A dual agent has responsibilities to both seller and buyer and must act in the interest of both parties. A dual agency is created when either one or two agents with the same brokerage represent both the buyer and the seller.

Due Diligence Period: The period in a real estate transaction following the acceptance of an offer, during which time the buyer has the right to carry out any inspections of the property that he or she deems necessary (including home appraisals or a home inspection). The due diligence period exists so that buyers can confirm all the facts pertaining to the sale, and occurs before a buyer and seller enter into a contract.

Escrow: In a real estate transaction, escrow refers to the funds paid by the buyer into an escrow account to be held until a specific date when the funds will be released to the seller, after all contingencies have been addressed and the deal is closed. The buyer's funds are placed in escrow to prove to the seller that the buyer is capable of making the payment, and to allow time to satisfy all the conditions of the sale. Once the escrow transfers the payment to the seller, the title is transferred to the buyer.

Escrow Company: The escrow or title company holds funds in escrow until all of the terms of both the buyer and seller are met. This company acts as a neutral third party in the transaction and holds the funds securely until the close of escrow.

Escrow Period: The duration of time during which the buyer's funds are held in escrow with the escrow or title company specified in the contract. During this period, the buyer performs his or her home inspections and obtains a loan, if necessary. When a home is "in escrow," this means that the sale is pending. The period usually lasts for 21-30 days, or, in a fast close situation, 14-21 days.

Estate Sale: A sale or auction held in one's home and run by an estate sale professional, with the purpose of selling unwanted furniture or household items and vacating a property before selling it. Estate sales are especially useful for anyone who is sizing down and want to get rid of certain possessions they no longer need. The major benefit of an estate sale is that the individual carrying out the sale for you will dispose of or donate any items that fail to sell, leaving you with an empty property.

Fair Market Value: The fair and accurate price for a home in an ideal situation. Many define fair market value as the highest price that a willing, but not compelled, buyer would pay for a home, and the lowest price a willing, but not compelled, seller would accept for the home. Ideally, a property's fair market value should reflect an accurate assessment of its worth.

First Alert (a.k.a. Property Alert): An online property listing database that locates properties of a specific description and alerts registrants as soon as such properties become available on your local market. Agents often set up their clients to receive daily First Alert updates via email, so that they are notified of new properties right away.

For Sale By Owner (FSBO): A circumstance in which a homeowner endeavors to sell his home himself, without the assistance or representation of a real estate agent. FSBO sales are typically disapproved of in our local market, since they rarely result in a successful sale and create unnecessary hassle for all parties involved due to the lack of knowledge on the part of the FSBO.

"Good Faith" Deposit (a.k.a. "Earnest Money" Deposit): A sum of cash—typically 3% of a home's purchase price in our area—that a buyer deposits into an escrow account maintained by a title or escrow company. This deposit goes toward the purchase price of the home and remains in the escrow account until the transaction closes.

Home Description: A depiction of a property posted online or published in print sources, written by a real estate agent, and used to advertise the property to potential buyers. Home descriptions are generally accompanied by professional photographs, and may sometimes contain misleading or overly laudatory jargon.

Home Inspection: A thorough examination of a property performed by a professional inspector that evaluates the mechanical and structural soundness of the property. Homebuyers often require that a home inspection be completed before they agree to purchase a home, as part of their contingency period. Home sellers may opt to perform a home inspection on their own home prior to market, in order to be aware of any preexisting problems that need to be addressed ahead of time; this is referred to as a pre-listing home inspection.

Housing Market: The supply and demand for houses in a particular location in which houses are purchased and sold. Housing markets can be defined by country, state, region, city, or neighborhood, and therefore differ depending on location. Like other markets, the housing market tends to fluctuate between high and low periods of activity.

HUD Settlement Statement: Also known as the HUD-1 Statement, the closing statement, or the settlement sheet, this document presents an itemized list of the funds paid at the closing of a real estate transaction. Funds listed might include: real estate agent commissions, loan fees, points, and initial escrow amounts. The totals calculated at the bottom of the statement reveal the seller's net proceeds and the buyer's net expenditure at closing. HUD refers to the U.S. Department of Housing and Urban Development, which provides the form.

Interest Rate: The cost of borrowing a lender's money. Interest rates on mortgages are determined by the going market rate. A borrower may opt to lower their rate by paying points. Points are prepaid interest. Points may be a tax deduction – check with your CPA.

Listing Agreement: A contract between a home seller and his or her real estate agent, detailing the terms of the partnership. The listing agreement names the agent and company as an authorized party able to represent the seller and attempt to sell the property, in exchange for a specified commission. Listing agreements also often include a beginning date and a termination date, the list price at which the property will be offered for sale, and the terms and conditions under which the commission shall be paid to the brokerage. Also referred to as a listing contract.

Loan Agent: Also known as a loan officer. The loan agent solicits loans for borrowers, represents a lending institution, and represents borrowers to the lending institution. Loan agents typically work for one particular bank.

Luxury Home: A luxury home—or luxury real estate—is often defined in the United States as any property that has an appraised value of $1 million or more. Some real estate agents, including Debbi DiMaggio and Adam Betta, specialize in the sale of luxury properties.

Micro-market: A term used to designate a very narrow and specific real estate market and its particular characteristics. We refer to the housing markets of Piedmont, Oakland, Berkeley and the various neighborhoods of the East Bay as micro-markets because their markets do not always follow the same trends as the larger markets around them (including that of San Francisco, Contra Costa County, or Marin), but operate according to their own standards, practices and values. It is important that an agent be informed on the goings on in her ultra-specific micro-market in order to best serve her clients in that region.

Mortgage: A legal document used by a borrower to pledge his or her property to a lender as security in order to obtain a loan; a debt instrument that the borrower is obliged to pay back in a set of installments. Homebuyers utilize mortgages to make large real estate purchases without having to pay the entire value of the home upfront.

Mortgage Broker: An intermediary who brings together mortgage borrowers and mortgage lenders, gathering necessary paperwork from a borrower and passing it along to the mortgage lender for approval. A mortgage broker collects an origination fee or some other form of compensation from the lender for his or her services. Mortgage brokers are not to be confused with mortgage bankers; mortgage brokers frequently facilitate transactions for mortgage bankers, who fund mortgages with their own funds.

Mortgage Lender: A person or company that provides real estate loans to borrowers. The lender then has a security interest in the property and charges interest on the loan amount. Lenders provide the money to the borrower at the closing table (unlike mortgage brokers, who simply offer the loan services of multiple lenders).

Multiple Listing Service (MLS): An online database compiling information on the real estate listings in a given area. Real estate agents who are members of the service help market and sell each others' houses, and clients benefit from the increased exposure among members.

Non-contingent: If an offer to buy a home is a non-contingent offer, this means that the buyer is prepared to purchase the home with no contingencies attached – meaning no further inspections, stipulations, or assurances are necessary. Non-contingent offers are the most appealing to sellers because they are hassle-free, and ensure that the buyer is qualified and able to complete the purchase.

Off-Market Sale (a.k.a. Private Sale): An off-market sale refers to a real estate transaction that occurs despite the fact that the subject property was never listed for sale on the market or on the Multiple Listing Service. In other words, it is when a property trades hands unofficially or confidentially and is not offered to the public. An off-market sale may occur for a variety of reasons. For example, Adam and I put our home up for sale back in 2009, just a few weeks before the mortgage meltdown hit the Bay Area. Needless to say, we took our home off the market. A few years later we were approached by an eager buyer with three children, anxious to get into the Piedmont School system. It worked out, and we sold our home – "off-market". Keep in mind, an off-market sale does not always go smoothly – there are many pros and cons. A few other scenarios include: a buyer's agent approaching a seller if the home appears to have all of the qualities that their buyer is seeking; or, a homeowner may tell their agent that they are open to selling if the right deal comes along. And the list goes on.

Offer: A buyer's invitation to make a deal with a seller regarding the purchase of the seller's home; a buyer's method of expressing interest to buy a property from a seller. In today's competitive real estate market, buyers need to put forth the highest price they are willing to pay in each offer that they make in order to prevail.

Offer Date: The specific day, specified by a seller and his or her agent, upon which offers to purchase the seller's home can be formally made. Offer dates are only set when there is noticeable interest in the property, and when multiple disclosure packets have been requested. On the offer date, the seller and seller's agent sit down with each buyer's agent one by one to hear offers at a designated time.

Offer Price: The amount offered by a potential buyer for a seller's home. An offer price generally represents whatever the buyer can afford, and therefore may be higher or lower than the seller's asking, or listing, price.

Open House: A scheduled period of time on a specified date during which a property is open and available to be viewed by potential buyers. In our area, most open houses are held on Sunday afternoons, and are widely advertised. Potential buyers can tour homes on their own or can attend open houses alongside their agent. A single home may be held open multiple times to attract the largest number of interested buyers or until the home is sold.

Pocket Listing: A pocket listing is a listing that is not on the MLS or on the open market. An agent who has a pocket listing will sign a listing agreement with a seller, with the understanding that the home is not to be marketed in the MLS, but will instead be advertised by word of mouth. This occurs if, for whatever reason, a seller prefers to sell his or her home privately. A pocket listing can be good or bad, depending on the situation; be wary, as you may undersell your home if you do not market it to the masses. However, if an absolutely perfect buyer comes out of the woodwork, this type of sale may be beneficial to both parties. Just beware, since these situations do not always work out. Take note: a home should still be market ready in order to entice a buyer to purchase that home off-market. Consult your agent or contact us to learn more.

Power of Attorney: A legal document providing one person (the "agent") with the ability to act on behalf of another person (the "principal"). For example, when one spouse cannot be present to sign the necessary contracts, legal documentation, and loan papers to buy a home, one spouse would be granted the power of attorney to sign on behalf of the other, absent spouse.

Preapproval: A process used to determine how much money a potential homebuyer will be eligible to borrow from a mortgage lender, prior to writing an offer. Preapproval gives buyers the ability to estimate what they can afford based on the size of the loan they can expect to receive. In our competitive local markets, any homebuyer absolutely must be preapproved for a loan before making offers to purchase a home.

Preemptive Offer: An offer to purchase a home that is submitted prior to the specified offer date. Preemptive offers tend to be significantly higher than the seller's asking price. Buyers make preemptive offers in order to attract the seller's approval before other potential buyers have even had the chance to see or submit an offer; for this reason, preemptive offers must be appealing enough to a seller to convince the seller to accept it.

Pre-qualification: A simple process, performed by a lender, that examines a potential borrower's income and expenditures in order to estimate a figure that the individual would likely be able to borrow; it is a rough estimate of the credit worthiness of a potential borrower. Pre-qualification is not as reputable or concrete as the similar but more rigorous preapproval process, and is therefore an insufficient demonstration in our market of a buyer's ability to purchase a home.

Ratified offer: A ratified offer is an offer that has been signed and executed by both buyer and seller.

Realtor®: A fully accredited real estate agent can be referred to as a Realtor® if he or she has joined the National Association of Realtor® (the NAR), agreeing to uphold its standards and code of ethics.

Referral: Referrals in real estate occur when one real estate agent recommends, or refers, a client to another agent. Agents refer clients who are looking to buy or sell in a different market (than their own) where the referred agent would undoubtedly have more local knowledge. Establishing cooperative networks with other agents in and around the state and even throughout the country enables us to develop a referral base in order that we may better serve our clients. It is important to us that we refer our clients to local specialists who are at the top of the market in their particular areas.

Referral Fee: Fees paid by one real estate agent to another for a client referral. A referral fee is a percentage of the commission paid to the agent who referred the client. For example, when we refer a client to an agent, we will receive a 20-25% referral fee, paid out of the referred agent's commission and vice versa.

Resale Value: The future value of a home or piece of property; the value of a home that was purchased in the past and is now going to be sold. Homeowners can always take steps to increase the eventual resale value of their home by staying on top of maintenance and upkeep, for example, or by making any additions or updates to the property that are appealing and add value. Other external factors that affect a home's resale value include the neighborhood and neighboring homes, the status of the local school district, and the climate of the housing market at the time of the sale.

Seller's Agent (a.k.a. Listing Agent): A real estate agent who represents the seller in a given transaction, partnering with him or her to sell his or her current home.

"Seller's Market": This term refers to the situation that arises when demand for homes exceeds supply. In such a situation, home sellers are at the advantage over home buyers and can use this to their advantage in price negotiations. Seller's markets often give rise to bidding wars, since buyers are highly competitive to secure properties. Also referred to as a "hot market." The current Bay Area real estate market is undeniably a seller's market.

Selling Price: While some define "selling price" as a synonym of "listing" or "asking price," a home's selling price can also refer instead to the price at which it actually sells in the end. Under this definition, then, the listing/asking price is determined by the seller and his agent, while the selling price is ultimately chosen by the buyer who makes the most competitive offer and secures the home.

Staging: Staging, or home staging, refers to the process of decorating and designing one's home—particularly the interior spaces—in a neutral and aesthetically pleasing manner, in order to increase its chances of appealing to the most buyers and selling for the highest possible price. Staging is carried out by professional home stagers who bring their own furniture and decorative items into to your home and arrange them in a pleasing way. Stagers also often help decide other aesthetic aspects of the home improvement process before a sale, such as the color to paint the walls or the type of fixtures or countertops to install.

Title: A legal written document that attests to an individual's lawful possession or ownership of a property.

Title Company: A company that provides comprehensive title insurance protection and professional settlement, escrow, and closing services for homebuyers, sellers, and many others. A title company's objective is to produce clear titles and enable the transfer of real estate. A title company represents a neutral third party in the real estate transaction. The practices and procedures of title companies vary from state to state and from region to region; indeed, not only do escrow procedures differ between northern and southern California, they also vary somewhat amongst the various counties. Title companies handle closings through escrow in northern California, whereas escrow companies and lenders handle them in southern California.

ACKNOWLEDGEMENTS

First off, we would like to thank Rob Bond, the Publisher of this work, for believing in us and pushing us to move forward with this guidebook. We are grateful for his insightful suggestions and critiques, and for the initial idea to collaborate with us on the creation of this book. Without his vision, this East Bay guide and the sequence of additional *Insider's Guides* to come would never have been written. Next we acknowledge Alison Mackey, our hardworking Editor, for keeping up with our whirlwind business and completing in one summer all of the research and composition involved in the creation of this book. Her enthusiastic "shadowing" of us while on the job, her grammatical skill, and her overall commitment to this project were essential to its successful completion. Many thanks also go to Annie Barbarika, our talented Graphic Designer, for her tireless efforts in making this publication so visually stunning, and to Kristen Malan for the perfect book cover.

We are grateful to Heidi Marchesotti, our Partner, who helped persuade us to move from the comfort of our last company to launch our current venture with her; also to Mindy Sun, silent Partner and good friend. Debbi would like to acknowledge Ron Kris, Don Woolhouse and Connie Rogers for their support and encouragement early on in her career. Adam would like to acknowledge his mentor, Gloria Corral; and, as always, our parents and in-laws, Vince and Midge DiMaggio and Carolyn Betta.

We are also indebted to several contributors, whose explanations and additions made the book as thorough as it is. These individuals are: Eric Ladrech, with Citibank in Piedmont; Quentin Bacon, professional SF Bay Area photographer (who is responsible for all of the impressive photographs featured in this book); and Renee Haugen, with First American Title Company. Acknowledgements are also due to Google Inc. for the use of their online-generated maps of our local communities.

Notes: